SCOTNOTES
Number 4

James Hogg's
The Private Memoirs and Confessions of a Justified Sinner

Elaine Petrie

Lecturer in English and Communication
Falkirk College of Technology

Association for Scottish Literary Studies 1988

Published by the
Association for Scottish Literary Studies
c/o The Department of English, University of Aberdeen
Aberdeen AB9 2UB

First published 1988

ISBN 0 948877 05 7

The Association for Scottish Literary Studies
is in receipt of subsidy from the Scottish Arts Council

CONTENTS

EDITORS' FOREWORD

The *Scotnotes* booklets are a series of study guides to major Scottish writers and literary texts that are likely to be elements within literature courses. They are aimed at senior pupils in secondary schools and students in further education colleges and colleges of education. Consequently it is intended that, wherever possible, each booklet in the series will be written by a person who is not only an authority on the particular writer or text but also experienced in teaching at the relevant levels in schools or colleges. Furthermore, the editorial board, composed of members of the Schools and Further Education Committee of the Association for Scottish Literary Studies, considers the suitability of each booklet for the students in question. In preparing the series, the editors are conscious of the fact that for many years there has been a shortage of readily accessible critical notes for the general student of Scottish literature; and they intend that *Scotnotes* will grow as a series at the rate of about two booklets a year to meet this need and provide students with valuable aids to the understanding and appreciation of the key writers and major texts within the Scottish literary tradition.

Lorna Borrowman Smith
Alan MacGillivray

ACKNOWLEDGEMENTS

In compiling this study guide I am especially indebted to the work of Barbara Bloedé, Ian Campbell, Douglas Gifford, David Groves, Gillian Hughes and Douglas Mack.

NOTE ON REFERENCES

The page references to the *Confessions* are to the Penguin English Library edition (P), published in 1983 and edited by John Wain, and to the Oxford World Classics edition (O), published in 1981 and edited by John Carey. Other references are to be found on page 53.

THE AUTHOR'S LIFE AND WORK

James Hogg was born in 1770 in the parish of Ettrick in Selkirkshire. His father Robert Hogg was a tenant farmer who also traded as a sheep dealer but, when young James was about six, his father was made bankrupt, having been let down by a business associate. The family were homeless until a neighbour took on the lease of their home and allowed Robert Hogg to stay on as his shepherd. This dramatic slump in the fortunes of the Hogg family meant that the young James had to contribute to the family income by working in the summer months as a cow-herd so that his education was largely informal.

There were two main influences in Hogg's early education: traditional folklore and religion. The parish of Ettrick had a proud history for it had once been in the charge of the Reverend Thomas Boston, an influential theologian. During Boston's ministry, church attendance rose dramatically and Boston's books and the sermons of Covenanting ministers were widely read across the country. The Hoggs were regular church attenders as Robert Hogg was an elder and he was also, for a time, the precentor, leading the congregation in the hymn singing. He read the Bible and other theological works extensively.

The young James Hogg was also introduced to some of the folklore and traditional song of the Borders by his mother, Margaret Hogg, and her brother William Laidlaw, who were both well versed in stories and songs. Margaret used to tell her sons 'tales of kings, giants, knights, fairies, kelpies, brownies, etc., etc.' but, as well as telling the boys tales of spirits and ghosts, she also taught them the Psalms — so that James could recite many of them by heart long before he could read.[1]

Hogg's relatives were not unusual in their committed interest in religion and in the controversial debates that surrounded it, for the hilly Border area had provided a refuge for many of the religious reformers known as Covenanters during the civil wars which had taken place almost a hundred years before Hogg's birth.

As a young man Hogg worked as a shepherd in Selkirkshire and Dumfriesshire. In his early twenties he became interested in literature and he soon tried writing songs and poems, some of which were published in *The Scots Magazine*. In 1801, he met Sir Walter Scott, who encouraged his writing to the point where, by 1807, Hogg had published a further book of poetry and a book on sheep diseases. In the meantime his farming ventures had not prospered and, when he found himself bankrupt in 1810, he determined to try his luck as a full-time writer in Edinburgh. He met with mixed commercial success though he made many useful friends and read widely. He published a collection of songs and set up a literary magazine, *The Spy*, which folded at the end of a year. He lived in Edinburgh till 1814, when he received a cottage from the Duke of Buccleuch. After that, he always divided his time between the country and Edinburgh, so that, in a way, he moved between two different worlds and lifestyles.

Hogg contined to blend farming and writing to the end of his life. He frequently experienced difficulty in getting his work printed as publishers such as Blackwood sometimes felt that Hogg's writing was too extravagant or too indiscreet for the genteel readers that provided the main book-buying market. This caused Hogg to experiment with many different styles and devices as he tried to present his work in a way that would be acceptable to this audience and to publishers. Between 1818 and 1824 he produced a series of novels, the last of which was the *Confessions*. Each of these works was disappointingly received and so Hogg turned back to poetry with the epic *Queen Hynde*, which sold poorly. As a result of these disappointments, Hogg confined himself to writing shorter pieces — stories, poems or songs — which could be published more easily.

Hogg married in 1820 and he and his wife had four children. When he died in November 1835, he was widely known as a writer but many of his contemporaries found it easier to patronise him as a Border curiosity than to accept the originality and strength of his work.

A large part of Hogg's work is made up of poems, songs, short stories or descriptive sketches which he sent in to popular magazines such as *The Scots Magazine, Blackwood's Edinburgh Magazine* and *Fraser's Magazine*. Many of these works were later collected and one of the best known series of articles forms *The Shepherd's Calendar*. This series is sometimes given the subtitle 'Tales Illustrative of Pastoral Occupations, Country Life and Superstitions', which describes its contents perfectly. Hogg's tales appealed both to the town dweller's nostalgic idea of the country and to the prevailing Romantic interest in nature and the life of those close to it.

In his own day Hogg's poems and songs were his most popular work. In the twentieth century his prose has received the greatest attention and praise. This partly reflects changing fashions in popular taste but it also shows the breadth of Hogg's talents. In fact he was not just a poet or a novelist: he wrote travel essays, short stories, popular songs and autobiography and produced editions of Jacobite songs and the poetry of Robert Burns.

He began by composing songs for the country folk he lived and worked with. Many of these pieces appeared in *The Forest Minstrel* (1810) and *Songs by the Ettrick Shepherd* (1831). His first collection of poems and songs, *Scottish Pastorals* (1801), deals with countryfolk without being parochial. One poem shows a very lively discussion between two shepherds about the taxes and the war with France, reminding us very effectively that, although world and national events sometimes seem remote, they do have an effect on the everyday life of the individual.[2] One of them, Geordie, is forced to kill his dog Dusty when he can no longer afford to pay the tax on dogs. Like Robert Wringhim, Geordie and Dusty become the victims of other people's values and beliefs.

A sharp-eyed observer of the community around him, Hogg was always keen to describe the old customs and traditions as he believed they were dying out. Sometimes he used legends or traditions as local colour in a story but often he wanted to explore the paradox that different people could interpret the same beliefs as 'superstition' or as actual 'true-life' occurrences. The contrasting attitudes represented the two different societies in which he moved. On the one hand there were the Borders where, although many of the old traditions had died out, storytelling, ballads and traditions about ghosts and avenging spirits were still part of everyday experience. On the other hand, there was Edinburgh, which had been the home of Enlightenment philosophy, an outlook that believed the world was an orderly place where everything could be explained rationally. It represented civilisation and harmony and there was no place for belief in irrational supernatural events. Hogg reflected both these outlooks at different times in his writing — even sometimes in the same work. Hogg's deep concern with tradition and with the past is also reflected in the fact that most of his major work is set in bygone times but he was not simply trying to provide local colour and a nostalgic picture of the world as it was. When the supernatural enters a story, it usually serves some spiritual or moral purpose.

LITERARY BACKGROUND TO THE *CONFESSIONS*

The Queen's Wake (1813), the poem which established Hogg's reputation, deals with the accession of Mary Queen of Scots and describes a competition among the bards of Scotland to show their queen the best minstrelsy of her new kingdom. There are references to traditional ballads but most of the bards perform poems composed by Hogg. Some of these are still regarded as Hogg's best work and they include 'Kilmeny', a haunting tale of a young girl spirited away to witness a mystical vision of paradise ('A land of love, and a land of light'), and 'The Witch of Fife', a vigorous and blackly humorous account of an old man who tries to join in with some witches.

Hogg continued to write poetry but never achieved the same commercial success again and so he turned more and more to prose, partly in longer book form and partly in the form of magazine pieces. *The Brownie of Bodsbeck* (1818), his first sustained prose work, is the one that most closely follows the normal format of the novel. It is set in 1685, when the Covenanters are in hiding across Scotland, pursued by the troops of Graham of Claverhouse, a man who gained a reputation as a savage, merciless persecutor. The book tells how Walter Laidlaw, a simple Border farmer, becomes embroiled in the war when he allows some Covenanters to hide on his land. His troubles are compounded by the fact that he suspects his daughter of being involved in witchcraft, although this is resolved when it is discovered that she also has been secretly helping the hiding Covenanters. Hogg's sympathies here are ranged on the side of the Covenanters, 'proscribed, imprisoned, and at last hunted down like wild beasts.' He does mention their 'fanaticism in religion' but this is far outweighed by the savagery of the Government troops. However, the real heroes of the story are Walter Laidlaw and his daughter who are moved to put themselves in danger to help others, regardless of politics or religion. Hogg makes it clear at several points in the story that a humane, commonsense attitude is more important than any particular religious viewpoint. Walter is not interested in the ins and outs of theological debate but he respects the Covenanters' right to hold their own views and is much more concerned with the immediate business of feeding the starving refugees. Walter is not irreligious but, like the Laird of Dalcastle, he does believe there is a time and place for religious observance.

The characters of *The Three Perils of Man* (1822) also find themselves caught between powerful, committed forces. On one level these forces are represented by the nobility of Scotland and England who engage in warfare in the name of 'chivalry'. These passionate and wilful people claim to be fighting for an ideal but in reality there is no good cause for the conflict. It is simply a lover's dare which sets in motion a war that leads to the casual slaughter of individuals as well as to large-scale carnage at the height of the siege. Meantime the story also deals with a small band of individuals who find themselves confronted by the supernatural powers of Michael Scott, the wizard of Aikwood. The dazzling climax of this part of the story comes when the wizard and Friar Roger Bacon engage in a trial of their powers of sorcery. Hogg carefully lets us see that Bacon's 'magic' is in fact a clever mixture of sleight-of-hand and science. He uses prisms and gunpowder to trick his audience and we are cosily congratulating ourselves on seeing through the sham when Michael Scott brings about the splitting of the Eildon Hills into three. Hogg offers no other explanation than that he has the help of the devil and Scott pays dearly for this assistance. All of a sudden, after the apparent triumph of rational explanation and scientific procedure, we are faced with a situation that demands belief in the supernatural and refuses to be explained away. Hogg returns again to this question of 'appearance' versus 'reality' in the *Confessions*.

The Three Perils of Man is written as if the author has found the story among the ancient manuscripts of 'old Isaac, the curate'. Hogg was fond of this narrative device and also of the presentation of apparently autobiographical accounts and brings the two together in the *Confessions*, while a number of other works give autobiographical accounts of eccentric characters. Some of these individuals, like Baillie Sydeserf,[3] are unattractive, conniving figures and many are pitted against powerful, compelling enemies whose lives are inextricably bound with their own. In 'The Adventures of Captain John Lochy', Lochy is befriended by Finlayson, a master of disguises who has great skill in persuading others to do his will and is sometimes taken by others to be the devil.[4] Between the years 1820 to 1825, Hogg worked on a group of these long 'autobiographical' accounts though many were not published until much later.

James Hogg was a most inventive and energetic writer whose

greatest love was to tell a story. He tried to carry on two professions since he could not afford to live by writing alone, but times were difficult for farmers and he depended on the extra money he could make from writing. His ceaseless experiment with new forms is due partly to his own creative imagination and partly to his need to get material published. If editors refused to print his work as it stood (they often objected that it was too frank about sexual matters), he would either salvage material, editing it and presenting it in another form, or he would try his hand at a different style of work.

RELIGIOUS BACKGROUND TO THE *CONFESSIONS*

In order to understand the ideas of the *Confessions*, it is helpful to know a little about the history of the Church of Scotland. The Church was frequently a subject of controversy and debate, inevitably becoming involved with politics when opposing sides adopted different sides in the religious debate — just as in modern politics different parties develop opposing lines on issues such as nuclear weapons.

In 1560 John Knox, a follower of the Swiss theologian John Calvin, proposed a plan for the reformation of the Church of Scotland which was accepted by a convention of the nobility and lairds. Later, in 1636-37 Charles I proposed changes to bring the Church of Scotland into line with the Church of England, including Archbishop Laud's plans for making the style of service closer to the Catholic form. This caused a national protest in the form of the National Covenant, a declaration signed in Greyfriars Church (1638) by nobility, barons, burgesses and ministers, who pledged themselves to defend their form of the Protestant religion. A General Assembly was called which abolished bishops and a Covenanting army was established. In 1643 the Solemn League and Covenant was signed with the English Puritans promising mutual support, and in the same year the Westminster Confession was signed which drew up the constitution for a unified Presbyterian church in England and Scotland. It was adopted in Scotland but not in England.

Civil war continued with many twists and turns till the 1650s when the Scots Covenanters decided to support Charles II; the English Puritans, under Cromwell, retaliated by inflicting heavy defeats on the Scots army. The Covenanters finally lost support in Scotland because, firstly, the traditional ruling classes came to resent control by the presbytery more than the threatened rule by king and bishops and, secondly, many people became sickened by the bloodshed.

After his restoration to the throne in 1660, Charles II reintroduced episcopacy (a reformed Church retaining bishops) but maintained a presbyterian structure in the kirk sessions. The compromise was an uneasy one and three hundred clergymen left their parishes because they declared themselves unable to accept bishops. The Lowland peasantry were sympathetic to the Covenanters — especially in Ayrshire, Dumfries and Galloway,

the central Borders and Fife — and open-air sermons, or con-
venticles, were held in these regions. The Government regarded these meetings as seditious and tried to put them down
by force. There were skirmishes and in 1679 extremists shot
Archbishop Sharp of St Andrews. Open war broke out and the
period became known as 'the Killing Time'. In 1685 James II
came to the throne and passed an Act of Parliament offering
religious tolerance to all creeds. This, coupled with James's own
open Catholicism, swung the balance for many. In 1688 the
nobility of both England and Scotland deposed James. After
the accession of William and Mary, the Presbyterians were in the
ascendant and Covenanting troops helped government forces to
put down Jacobite opposition to the new king and queen.

A new church constitution was worked out and ratified in
1690 by William. This presbyterian constitution restored the
General Assembly and abolished bishops but the Church was
now subject to Parliament. Five hundred old-style clergy split
away to form the Episcopal Church of Scotland, while a number
of extreme, diehard Covenanters also stayed outside the established church. One such group were the Cameronians.

As in any debate, there were varying degrees of belief, so
that some took moderate views and other factions were
more extreme. The question of *predestination* became a heated
battleground. Its supporters argued that since God knows everything, it must follow that right from the beginning of time he
has known who will be saved (that is, *elect* or *justified*) and who
will be damned (or *reprobate*). Some believed that a proper repentance for sins would earn God's forgiveness. You could perhaps try to ensure your salvation by leading a pure life and
doing good works. The Antinomians, on the other hand, — and
this includes the Reverend Robert Wringhim — believed that
man could not alter God's judgement in any way. Good works
could not 'buy' salvation — the individual must simply have faith
in the grace of God. It follows that, since one cannot alter the
predestined decision about who has been 'chosen' by God,
someone who is destined for heaven would not be deprived of
salvation because of any mistakes made on earth. Gil-Martin
persuades Robert that if this is true, the elect may not even
need to obey the normal moral laws; they are in a sense above
them. Paradoxically, the justified may be free to sin.

But how can people be sure that God has chosen them? For
most individuals, lacking that supreme self-confidence, the idea
of predestination must have meant an agony of uncertainty,

even moments of despair, especially as orthodox religious observance seemed to stress the sinfulness of the average individual.

The restored General Assembly introduced stricter observances to reduce backsliding and the Church continued this severe approach for many years. Sundays were to be spent in religious worship either at home or in church and there were severe punishments for Sabbath-breaking, a crime which included going for a walk or whistling on a Sunday. Servants had to have testimonials vouching for their Christian behaviour in order to change job and any sexual freedom outside marriage had to be answered for in front of the whole congregation. However, from 1762 to 1780 the Moderate party held power in the Assembly and the influence of Enlightenment philosopy began to spread, with its spirit of free enquiry and more liberal attitudes.

In the meantime there had also been controversy in political circles. The Scottish Parliament had for some time been rather ineffectual and was usually under the control of the monarch's advisers but, in the reign of William, it became more independent. This led to conflict with the Crown over matters such as trade in the colonies. Thereafter the English Parliament tried to exert control and, in 1703 and 1704, the Scottish Parliament threatened to disband the existing links with England. However, pressures towards full union were considerable, especially if the Protestant succession was to be secured. These were the sort of issues that were being discussed in the Scottish Parliament in Edinburgh when the Wringhims and Colwans met in the city.

CONFESSIONS: STRUCTURE AND STYLE

STRUCTURE

The structure is one of the most strikingly original things about the *Confessions*. The book is in three parts with the Editor's Narrative forming an elaborate frame round Robert's memoir. To add further mystery, Hogg published the book anonymously, hoping to imply it had been written by someone from Glasgow — and indeed part of the action takes place in that city. (Hogg had been involved in a similar hoax in 1817 when he wrote the first draft of 'The Chaldee Manuscript', a satirical spoof, written in the style of the Old Testament, satirising the publishers in Edinburgh and the setting up of *Blackwood's Magazine* in particular. James Hogg wrote the original draft and two young lawyers, John Lockhart and John Wilson, revised the document till it was practically libellous and had to be suppressed. Lockhart is introduced at the end of *Confessions* and Wilson may have been a model for the Editor.)

The frame introduces the Memoir, offers us ways of interpreting the events and makes the story seem real by including real-life characters and events to lend authenticity. Like the narrator in 'Tam o' Shanter', the writer wants us to believe we are reading 'a tale o' truth'.

The first part of the Editor's Narrative introduces the background information and the main characters. It generates sympathy for the Colwans and creates an air of rational objective investigation. Robert's Memoir then offers a highly emotional and subjective account of some of the same events, adding some that the Editor could not trace. The final section takes us back to the 'modern' period and adds further background 'evidence' to establish a sense of 'normality', the here-and-now, while still suggesting lurid possibilities of things beyond nature.

The use of both an autobiography and a fictional Editor prevents the reader from thinking of Hogg as the author, encouraging the illusion that this is a 'true' account. The resulting story-within-a-story pattern is mirrored in several ways inside the book itself when different people describe the same events differently and stories get passed on. The Auchtermuchty story was actually told by Lucky Shaw, then retold via Samuel Scrape, Robert and the Editor. This device is used in folk tradition where a story-teller always claims the story is true saying that it came from somebody else who saw it happen. Hogg adapts this to remove the usual all-seeing omniscient narrator and force the reader to weigh up the evidence and judge accordingly.

As well as paired narratives, the book sets various characters up to be compared and contrasted. This adds to the overall sense of balance and intricate patterning. The final design is ambitious and many details are echoed in different parts of the book, shedding new light on earlier events and colouring the attitude to new ideas.

STYLE

The language of the book varies according to the nature of the action and of the speaker. Hogg uses Latinate vocabulary, inversion, circumlocution and elaborate sentence structure in the opening of the Editor's Narrative to suit his highly educated style — see the last sentence in the first paragraph (P: 29; O: 1). Bessy Gillies, John Barnet and Hogg the shepherd use rich Scots dialect, demonstrating their down-to-earth commonsense. Thus Hogg is more concerned with his 'paulies' and 'stotts' (P: 236; O: 247) while Barnet uses proverbs and irony that give his listeners 'a kind o' yerk, an' that gars them wince' (P: 115; O: 104). The Wringhim household all uses ornate Biblical prose even in domestic situations, reminding us that they are more concerned with the forms of religion than with its practice. Robert's use of this Biblical style in the opening of the Memoir strikes a hysterical tone with the use of words like 'vengeance', 'tremble' and 'blood' (P: 109; O: 97) warning us of the actions to come.

Even characters who only make brief entries into the story, like the jailer and Linton the printer, make strong impressions because of their individual linguistic style. It seems the jailer is an Aberdonian by his use of 'fat' and 'fa' for 'what' and 'who' as much as by his interest in money (P: 153-4; O: 149-50). Linton's good-natured distraction is conveyed by short phrases and repetition (P: 213; O: 220). Gil-Martin's use of language is especially precise and shows very careful manipulation of words and ideas. See, for example, his references to his shape-changing, his Bible and the fact that his servants *think* they are Christians (P: 132, 142; O: 124-5, 136).

Throughout the text apparently casual words and phrases (particularly those referring to demons, devils and fiends), which seem entirely spontaneous in context, act cumulatively to generate a supernatural atmosphere and develop our impressions, particularly of Robert and his changing relationship with Gil-Martin.

CONFESSIONS: CHARACTERS AND THEMES

CHARACTERS

Robert is the most anti-heroic of all anti-heroes. The Editor's Narrative convinces us that he is a cowardly figure and there seems to be nothing to offer in his defence. He pursues George, involves him in scuffles and is responsible for his and other deaths. At first the Memoir makes things worse. He is spiteful; he lies; causes M'Gill's expulsion and Barnet's dismissal; he murders Blanchard and George; he commits suicide. Furthermore, it seems likely he murdered his mother, seduced a girl and ruined her family; yet all the time he continues to rely on his promised salvation.

Paradoxically, the Memoir, while revealing Robert's crimes, also allows the reader to develop a certain sympathy for him. First, it is told from Robert's point of view and uses the first person ('I'). This puts us in Robert's place and allows us to identify more easily with him. In this way we learn how and what Robert is thinking, something the Editor can never truly do. From this we can learn how completely Robert relies on his interpretation of predestination and the immunity of the elect. We may not be able to condone his ideas or actions but at least we can see how he arrives at them.

The second advantage of the Memoir is that it shows how lonely Robert is. In effect, he has no father nor any affectionate home life. This isolation and the stress on religious debate make him more and more introspective and obsessed with the state of his salvation. He fails to get this into perspective with the business of living. He is too involved in splitting hairs in debate (P: 110; O: 98-9) and too repressedly afraid of women (P: 123; O: 113) to understand ordinary human behaviour. Hogg wants us to see this lack of proportion as harmful. Robert's isolation makes him especially receptive to Gil-Martin's flattery. Gil-Martin is the only independent 'person' to take any interest in him and this is intensified by the fact that he seems important (a 'great prince') in his exotic clothing, repeatedly stressing how important Robert is to him.

The ease with which Gil-Martin manipulates Robert also shows how impressionable Robert is. He never takes a moral stand on his own but is thoroughly dependent, first on the

Reverend Mr Wringhim and then on Gil-Martin. His physical cowardice ties in with his moral weakness. He sees force as the only means of securing his wishes and yet he is unable to make any sort of a stand, finding a perverse pleasure in grovelling in blood and dirt. His breakdown is inevitable.

Robert's one potential virtue is his naivety or innocence which appears in his meetings with Gil-Martin. To the reader it is laughable that Robert does not realise that all Gil-Martin's utterances are double-edged and it is even more amusing that he should imagine his friend is the Czar of Russia (although Peter the Great did come to Britain to learn about ship-building). Because of this naivety, we are able to feel some sympathy for Robert. We must also have pity for the real fear and panic he feels as his life and his mind seem to disintegrate around him. By the end, he does have doubts about Gil-Martin but he can never bring himself to admit what has happened as that means the frightening admission that he has sinned and may be damned.

Gil-Martin: one unusual feature of this book is that we do not meet Gil-Martin, an important influence on the action, until quite late on. Mysterious, anonymous figures are referred to at various points and the supernatural is hinted at in Mrs Calvert's description of the events leading to George's murder (P: 90-1; O: 73-4). The mood of hysteria is increased when Robert's companion is seen to resemble George (P: 96-9; O: 81-4). Only now do we hear the name Gil-Martin for the first time (P: 103; O: 89). The reader has been prepared for something sinister and treacherous so that when 'a young man of a mysterious appearance' (P: 125; O: 116) appears in Robert's Memoir, looking like Robert and claiming to be his 'second self' or 'brother', the reader already knows this person will let Robert down.

Gil-Martin's double-edged references to God, the Bible and Robert's religious views also alert the reader to his likely identity but if Gil-Martin *is* the devil, Hogg's representation of him is highly effective. He avoids the old traditional picture of a horned monster and presents a suave, attractive double-dealer, the sort that anyone might entertain unaware. His conversations with Robert are carefully developed so that he first overcomes his fears by flattery (P: 126-7; O: 117-8) then gradually becomes more insistent and haughty (P: 140-1, 162-3, 187; O: 133-4, 160, 188-9) till his full final horror is revealed to Robert (P: 219-21, 225, 230; O: 227-9, 235, 240). Robert begins by longing for his company but ends by fleeing.

He changes his form to reflect the appearance of the person

he studies (P: 132-3; O: 124-5) and at various times takes the shape of Robert, George, the Reverend Mr Blanchard and Thomas Drummond. In a sense he, like Robert, lacks a real identity of his own and defines himself by taking on the views and shape of others. Gil-Martin then persuades Robert to accept these distorted versions of reality. Notice that the vision of Robert that haunts George is likened to a demon and its 'hideous malignity' reflects Gil-Martin's ability to accentuate Robert's dislike for George (P: 60; O: 37-8). Gil-Martin's references to God contain a mixture of resentment and a tacit acknowledgement of his own eternal damnation (P: 126, 132; O: 118, 125). While there is humour at the black irony in the conversations between Gil-Martin and Robert, Gil-Martin remains a humourless figure (P: 139; O: 132-3).

The Editor: it is sometimes easy to forget that the Editor himself is a fictional character since he conveys his viewpoint with such authority, judging events and colouring our responses. Hogg's role as author slips into the background, contradicted by his appearance as a character at the end. The first page of the narrative shows the Editor as a pedantic gentleman with Tory sympathies. He despises Robert's physical weakness and cowardice (P: 48, 64; O: 23-4, 43) and supports the Colwans, approving their carefree, pleasure-seeking lives as gentlemanly and glossing over those of their actions that might seem unattractive. He *appears* to be objective but he is predisposed to favour the Colwans.

The Editor believes in the power of reason and he represents the 'modern' viewpoint against the superstitious attitudes associated with the uneducated peasants Robert meets. Despite his rational education, it is the Editor who is left confused about what actually happened and how to evaluate it.

The Laird of Dalcastle, the elder George Colwan, is shown to us as an apparently attractive character. He is jolly, enjoys drinking and dancing at the wedding and wins our approval because, after his first incredulous outburst, he does not criticise his wife's interest in religion but merely says that her intense interest allows her to get things out of proportion (P: 32; O: 4-5). He gets a lot of sympathy through the slapstick comedy of the marriage and because of his image as a well-to-do, easy-going sort of chap. He is certainly the Editor's idea of a well-meaning country gentleman, not too godly but with the right intentions. His main concern is to live and let live in comfort, protecting his own interests. Though sympathetic towards the

Presbyterian movement, he took no action for them in the wars for fear of losing his lands. Later, alarmed by the extreme views of the Wringhims, he takes part in politics *against* Presbyterianism.

George seems to succeed naturally in life. Doted on by his father and Miss Logan, he is popular with his fellows. The Editor reports him as being 'generous and kind-hearted' (P: 43; O: 18) and he fits the image of the non-intellectual, athletic, man-about-town. He and Robert present a complementary picture — they are two sides of the same coin and one of a series of such parallels in the book. In this respect the book is a classic interpretation of the archetypal struggle between two brothers, the Cane and Abel myth. But it would be a mistake to see George as ideal; he is quick-tempered, insults his own mother's name in public, frequents brothels and quarrels with Drummond as well as Robert. Like Robert he also fails to execute all his good intentions — his trip to see his friend's sweetheart diverts him from his intention to pray and he lets his plan to seek out Robert and ask his forgiveness slip from him.

Bell Calvert's perspective on the Colwan family also adds an important dimension to our picture of George and his father. They have appeared attractive characters to us and we know that the Editor is sympathetic to them and that Mrs Logan is passionately dedicated to their memory yet Bell, the first apparently unbiased witness who actually seems to have been familiar with them, says she knew them both 'and never for any good' (P: 79; O: 60). On the other hand, George does display a sensitive temperament when he communes with nature on Arthur's Seat and he is, as Robert admits, quick to apologise and ask for reconciliation.

Lady Dalcastle, Rabina Colwan, is overshadowed by the Reverend Robert Wringhim and seems to have little character of her own. She appears cold and strait-laced in the wedding description although it might be worth remembering that the laird seems to be much older than she is (and drunk!). It does seem that part of the coldness which allows her to reject one son and leave the other unchristened is due to the fact that she herself was rejected as a child and when she returns after the wedding. Her only pleasure is in complicated arguments about religion (P: 42; O: 16) and the only emotion she displays is petty jealousy when Arabella Logan takes her place. She does show some anxiety for Robert's well-being but it seems this is often expressed in moral or religious terms, presumably as concern about his salvation. Notice that, apart from Gil-Martin, she is the only one who interprets absolute predestination as meaning 'that a justified person can do no wrong' (P: 39; O: 13) and she may have placed the idea in Robert's mind. Robert comes to resent her, feeling stifled by her affection for him (P: 183; O: 184). She is also a rival for the Reverend Mr Wringhim's attentions and senses that Gil-Martin is a threat (P: 128-9; O: 120-1). Robert also dislikes her because Wringhim has taught him that the physical beauty of women is a temptation towards sin. In his rational moments Robert must be aware that if he is Wringhim's son, as he wishes to be, then his parents are both adulterers and hypocrites yet it is easier for him to excuse Wringhim Senior by believing that his mother is wicked and the real culprit.

The Reverend Robert Wringhim seems to be the one human character without any saving graces (ironically enough!) and the best character summaries are supplied by the laird (P: 40-1; O: 15) and Barnet (P: 115-16; O: 104-5). It is Wringhim's distortion of religion, 'making distinctions in religion where none existed' (P: 42; O: 16) that blinkers and warps Robert. His brooding on the darker side of the Scriptures (sin and the more lurid psalms) generates Robert's obsessions with sin, corruption and vengeance. His hypocrisy is illustrated by his criticism of the laird and Miss Logan when it seems likely that he is Robert's real father and therefore an adulterer. Besides this, he is self-centred and complacent, believing that he is superior to his servant Barnet. The final sign that he is an untrustworthy character is that Gil-Martin and he seem so compatible and Gil-Martin leaves Robert for a time to be near the minister (P: 183, 185; O: 184, 186). Robert longs to do soldierly acts, as this will out-do the ministerial work of Wringhim Senior, which he sees as essentially passive and ineffective. However, the minister does play a significant role in the politics of the day and though the Editor tries to make a joke of it, he has to admit that Wringhim was 'of real use to the heads of the presbyterian faction' (P: 45; O: 20). This mixing of politics and religion feeds Wringhim's pride but Hogg shows that the manipulation that goes on in political and legal affairs is corrupt. The truly sincere Christian characters are those like Barnet, Blanchard and the cottagers who stay well away from these matters.

Arabella Logan, the laird's housekeeper, devoted companion and probable mistress, is a woman of good family fallen on hard times. (She may be a Catholic since her family's estates were confiscated during the Covenanting wars.) She is an emblem of warmth and devotion since she devotes herself to the Colwan family, adoring George and carrying on the laird's mission to uncover George's murderer. In these ways she has been more of a 'real' mother and wife than Lady Dalcastle who fills these roles in name only. Arabella Logan is later given the title 'Mrs' simply because this was the title given as a mark of respect to all women of mature years, regardless of whether they were married or not.

Her passionate nature means that she is impressionable and liable to snap decisions. This can lead her to hysteria and it also poses her problems when she meets Bell Calvert. Can she set aside her pride and her right of possession over the stolen goods and trust in her fellow human being? Unlike some of the other characters in the book, having chosen hastily at the first test, she is allowed to change her decision and free Bell Calvert.

There are significant parallels between Mrs Logan and Bell Calvert. Both are called Arabella and both have been dependent for their livelihood on the friendship of men. Bell Calvert points out that in fact she is in some respects a more fulfilled, more effective human being than Mrs Logan. She has a daughter and has known a mother's feelings, whereas Mrs Logan has been subordinated to her 'old unnatural master' (P: 79; O: 60). She also reminds Mrs Logan of her unmarried state and dubious position in the Colwan ménage: 'But as for you, you have never been any thing!' (P: 79 O: 61) and she charges Mrs Logan with the sort of sanctimonious religious hypocisy that we have hitherto only associated with the Wringhims when she says that her visitor will not forgive her but will ask God to do so. From this alone it should be clear that Hogg is not concerned with the failings of any one sect or party but with basic human flaws that run right across the divisions imposed on society.

Bell Calvert's past is lurid and dramatic and she is a mystery. She has been imprisoned for theft and swindling, has been whipped, forced to beg and has twice earned money by prostitution. Despite this, she does not cringe or beg Mrs Logan for help but addresses her as an equal. She does not seem to fear death so much as the indignity of death by hanging — the idea of it 'rends to flinders a soul born for another sphere than that in which it has moved' (P: 78; O: 59). Drummond also feels that she has the manner of a lady of 'the first class of society' (P: 89; O: 72). Bell Calvert proves that she retains some honour by refusing to trade her life for information and, of the three main female characters, she is the one who emerges with the most authority. Yet again we are forced to recognise that we cannot judge character by first appearance and Mrs Logan, who makes this mistake by saying that Bell's daughter would be better off without her mother, nearly loses the key to the murder mystery by her hasty assessment.

The fact that such a dignified and sympathetic character has been driven to commit 'crimes of utter desperation' (P: 80 O: 61) reminds the reader that each of us may be more vulnerable than we imagine and her claim that her crimes have been great but her sufferings greater (P: 80; O: 61) could be applied to other characters in the book.

John Barnet, the minister's servant, provides a 'moderate' alternative to the Wringhims' 'sublime and ridiculous sophistry' (P: 113; O: 101) and helps to 'test' young Robert. He knows of the boy's lies and hypocrisy and also exposes the vanity and complacency of the minister. Barnet displays wit and integrity in his confrontation with Wringhim (P: 115-7; O: 104-7) and a sense of fair play in dealing with Robert (P: 122; O: 112-3). He is one of those characters who seem refreshingly real and down-to-earth after the lurid extremes the Wringhims present.

The Reverend Mr Blanchard demonstrates the benign face of Protestant Christianity. The meetings with Blanchard are part of the testing of Robert. By disregarding Blanchard's humane, moderate viewpoint, Robert embarks on the commission of cardinal crime: murder. Blanchard gives Robert important warnings about Gil-Martin, Gil-Martin's dread of religion and the way in which Scripture can be quoted for bad ends (P: 138; O: 131). Blanchard's sermon about the power of free will, arguing that people can choose good or evil actions contradicts Robert's and Gil-Martin's belief that actions are preordained by God (P: 141; O: 135). This makes him a threat to Gil-Martin's influence over Robert which depends on Robert's belief that he is predestined to be saved and can therefore do no wrong.

Samuel Scrape, called Penpunt, Robert's servant, is called after the village of Penpunt in Dumfriesshire, an area particularly associated with the Covenanters. Penpunt belongs to one of the more extreme Presbyterian sects, the Cameronians, and he tells Robert two humorous parables. The first reminds us that human nature is flawed since even a strict Cameronian will not let principles deprive him of profit (P: 191-2; O: 194-5). The second shows that the devil, disguised as a minister, can preach religion to his own ends (P: 194-9; O: 197-203). Penpunt thus represents a down-to-earth viewpoint to contrast with Robert's extreme religious principles. He expresses the attitudes of the common villagers and warns that those who make the most show of being religious are not always the most trustworthy.

M'Gill, like George, is popular and successfully holds the position Robert aspires to. The reader is horrified at the pleasure Robert takes in his devious plans to bring down his rival. In a psychological interpretation, the echo of M'Gill's name in Gil-Martin's suggests Robert's guilty conscience at work. On a supernatural level, the fact that Robert is so ready to believe that M'Gill's success is gained through witchcraft probably makes him susceptible to the approaches of evil powers.

THEMES

The themes are often explored through comparison of paired characters: Robert and George; the laird and the Reverend Robert Wringhim; Bell Calvert and Arabella Logan. Hogg's main target is hypocrisy and he has least sympathy for characters who assume that they are superior to their fellows. His attack on the Wringhims is based on the fact that they distort religion in order to puff up their own importance. Hogg mistrusts any kind of fanatical or blinkered viewpoint and shows how this leads to confusion and corruption in the law courts and in politics as well as in the religious debate. Characters such as Bell Calvert and Mrs Logan show that the morally 'respectable' characters are not the automatic custodians of justice. The story also proves that, whereas the Editor and other representatives of rationalism find themselves confused at the end of the book, the supernatural will in the end bring due punishment. It is the down-to-earth country characters, John Barnet and the cottagers, who triumph by displaying kindness to Robert when necessary but also an immediate sense of what is right and wrong.

The 'story-within-a-story-within-a-story' structure with its emphasis on doubles (two generations of George Colwans and Robert Wringhims; two Arabellas; the apparitions) poses a more fundamental question about the gap between appearance and reality and the nature of absolute objective 'truth'. It is developed into the attack on hypocrisy but also demonstrates the difficulty for the individual in making sense of a changing world, an appropriate theme for a novel set in a period of party strife between the persecution of the Covenanters and the Jacobite Risings.

THE EDITOR'S NARRATIVE (1)

Plot Summary

The Editor gives the family background to the story and describes the wedding and early married life of the Laird of Dalcastle and Rabina Orde. Two sons are born: George, the eldest, is brought up by the Laird and his companion, Miss Arabella Logan; Robert is brought up by his mother and her minister, the Reverend Robert Wringhim, whose name the boy adopts. The boys meet in Edinburgh in 1704 and are immediately embroiled in conflict, involving the opposed political parties in the city. George is tried for attacking Robert on Arthur's Seat but witnesses prove that Robert followed George there. George is killed in mysterious circumstances and his father dies of grief. Robert inherits the estate of Dalcastle. Miss Logan tries to prove that Lady Dalcastle and the Wringhims have murdered George. She enlists the help of Bell Calvert and the pair find Robert accompanied by a strange young man who seems to know what they are after and who looks uncannily like the dead George. Bell recognises Robert as the man who murdered George and the women report him to the authorities. When the officers arrive to arrest him, Robert has already vanished.

Introducing the Editor and the Colwan marriage

The Editor begins in an authoritative, somewhat pedantic way, listing the various ways Dalcastle can be spelt. We quickly picture him, shut up in his study, poring through old books and records. He has a slightly dismissive attitude towards the people whose lives he is dissecting, describing the events as 'motley adventures' (P: 29; O: 1) and he writes in the weighty, long-winded style of a judge, using a good deal of inversion and circumlocution.

He introduces his subjects in a series of swift thumbnail sketches touched with irony. The laird is 'a droll, careless chap', who complacently believes that he is 'living in most cordial terms' (P: 30; O: 2) with man and God alike. His young wife, far from being a 'gay dame from the city', is 'the most severe and gloomy of all bigots', nursing beliefs that are 'overstrained and deformed', while the Reverend Robert Wringhim is not 'the good parson' of conventional fiction but a 'flaming predestinarian divine' whose ideas 'were so rigid, that they became a stumbling-block to many of his brethren' (P 30; O: 2). Each of these characters is in some sense isolated by his or her beliefs. Even the laird's 'cordiality' means that he hasn't taken one side or the other in the political and religious debates. It quickly becomes clear that this marriage of convenience is destined to be unhappy – the laird gets drunk, cavorts energetically and kisses all the pretty girls in the room whereas the lady seems to despise the man she has married to achieve the social prestige of calling herself 'Lady Dalcastle' (P: 31; O: 3).

The marriage scenes are extremely funny in a broad bur-lesque sort of way and though no character is shown in a very good light, the carefree, tipsy laird seems to speak with the voice of moderation when he says continual prayer makes a farce of religion (P: 32; O: 5). The emotive words 'bigot' and 'hypocrite' ensure that the lady comes off worse but, without the Editor's ironically detached humour, these scenes might have been a good deal less amusing. The Editor glosses over the young bride's alarm when she is faced by so much that is un-familiar on her wedding night and we may already wonder just how fair and unbiased he really is.

Rabina's return to her parents' home shows that she has never experienced real happiness. Her father 'never loved or ad-mired her greatly' (P: 35; O: 8) and we may remember that she was first described by the Editor as the '*reputed* daughter' of Baillie Orde (my italics). This suggested illegitimacy seems to be confirmed by the laird who later says that Robert is 'third in a direct line who had all been children of adultery', adding that such individuals were 'born half deils' (P: 67; O: 46). Rabina's treatment by her father may explain her readiness to enter into an unhappy marriage and, since Rabina herself has been so effect-ively disowned by her family, we can perhaps begin to under-stand her ability to reject her own son George. The only animated moments she experiences are in her 'wire-drawn' religious de-bates (P: 37; O: 10) but, when she and Wringhim discuss types of faith, making a symbolic thirteen and not twelve as the Editor says, they are concerned with listing and dissecting different categories rather than with faith itself (P: 38; O: 12).

It is significant that the lady retires to the upper part of the house for, throughout the book, the Wringhim doctrines are de-scribed ambiguously as 'high' and 'elevated'. The Wringhims may aspire to heaven but they have also lost any down-to-earth ability to relate their beliefs to daily life. Furthermore, towards the end of the book we are reminded that the devil is also called 'the prince o' the air' (P: 194; O: 197).

The theme of hypocrisy is explored through her curiosity and jealousy at Arabella Logan's role as the laird's companion. She at once suspects Miss Logan of stealing and is scandalised by the 'intimacies' she is sure are taking place. Ironically the Reverend Mr Wringhim notes that 'To the wicked, all things are wicked; but to the just, all things are just and right' (P: 39; O: 13) and Lady Dalcastle significantly interprets this as meaning 'that a justified person can do no wrong!'.

The confrontation between Wringhim and the laird develops the theme further, again with great humour. The Editor coyly tells us that the laird and Miss Logan are intimately poring over a book together and are rather startled when the Reverend Mr Wringhim burst in and accuses the laird of adultery. The laird catches the tone of religious debate and delivers a key assessment of Wringhim (P: 40-1; O: 15), returning the accusation of adultery.

The Editor prevents us from hearing the reply but although Wringhim clearly believes his rebuke has been successful, Miss Logan becomes the laird's housekeeper. Thus we have an example in miniature of the same events being retold in two different ways: the Editor relates them to us, emphasising the laird's speech while Wringhim and Lady Dalcastle report the event as a victory over the laird. Colwan's speech also introduces ideas of disease that prepare us for the distorted view of the world and the diseased intellect that we will find in Robert's memoir.

A sexual encounter between Wringhim and Lady Dalcastle is implied (P: 42; O: 16-7) and the events of the next few years are quickly glossed over, though we learn that Robert, from the moment of his birth, is a nameless outcast. The laird refused to take part in the christening and so the baby remained 'an alien from the visible church for a year and a day' till Wringhim baptises him in his own name (P: 43; O: 18). The two boys grow in opposite directions, with George excelling in 'all that constitutes gentility in deportment and appearance' (P: 44; O: 19). (We shall see just exactly what this means later.) Robert, on the other hand, has 'ungovernable passions' but is apparently diligent in school and is taught to hate the Colwans.

Meantime, his encounter with the Wringhim household pushes the laird into political commitment. From being unattached to either side, leaning publicly towards the monarchy

(James II, a Catholic, was on the throne when Colwan became the laird), but 'a secret favourer' (P: 44; O: 19) of the Covenanters, the laird moves to open support of the Jacobites and Episcopalians against the Covenanters. The Wringhim and Colwan households are now diametrically opposed in all possible ways.

The conflict between the brothers

The book now concentrates on the rivalry between the brothers, throwing the emphasis on George whose position as a popular gentleman about town gains the support of the Tory Editor. Structurally, it is important that George's case should be presented well here as the Memoir will present Robert's case emotively in his own voice.

Unlike the solitary Robert, George is the centre of a large, admiring crowd. His expertise at sport makes him 'the king of the game' (P: 46; O: 21) while Robert is described as a 'devilish-looking youth' or a 'moody and hellish-looking student' who interrupts the game by jostling his brother. Robert haunts George in the way that he is later haunted by a figure who looks like George. It is when an unnamed member of the party swears that Robert actively begins to taunt George and, equally curiously, it is 'a stranger' who tells George who Robert is. Could this be Gil-Martin? George's anger at Robert goads him into saying Robert is not a Colwan, thus insulting not only Robert bùt his own mother. He quickly realises that he has behaved badly but this action allows Robert to gain confidence, spurning Robert's apologies. Covered in dirt and almost begging to be beaten, Robert appears disgustingly abject as well as cowardly and ungenerous.

The resulting riot at the Black Bull shows first of all the confusion that results as two parties hotly contest opposing views, with each side ready to believe the worst of the other. The same events are made to appear slightly different, depending on which side is telling the story so that we are left to wonder whether absolute truth can ever exist. Yet again an anonymous individual adds fuel to the fire by shouting 'Treason' (P: 50; O: 26). In the middle of it all, it is the landlord, concerned for the safety of his house, who cynically weighs the odds and plays one party off against another. In the end the irony is that the opposing groups in the inn wind up fighting together against the mob outside.

The chief result is that the Reverend Mr Wringhim issues a

violent curse in the form of verses taken from the metrical version of Psalm 109:

> Set thou the wicked over him,
> *And upon his right hand*
> *Give thou his greatest enemy,*
> *Even Satan, leave to stand.*   (P 55; O: 32)

The reference to 'his mother's sin' and pleasure in 'cursing' seem
to echo the events surrounding Gorge at the tennis match. Certainly George does later find himself jeered at by the crowd and
haunted by Robert, who always stands on his right, but divine
justice ensures that this curse works two ways and *both* George
and Robert will find supernatural figures attending them.

George begins to learn what it is like to be lonely and un-
popular as his friends drift away. He becomes confused by the
'darting looks' (P: 58; O: 36) of the apparition and its uncanny
ability to read his mind. When his good intention of going to
church 'to attend divine worship' becomes perverted into going
to 'Grey-Friars' Church to look at his friend's sweetheart, the
apparition appears, just as the psalm prophesied. By this time
we no longer need the hint that 'the attendance of that brother
was now become like the attendance of a demon on some devoted being that had sold himself to destruction' (P: 60; O: 37) to
make us guess that we are dealing with something more than
natural, something supernatural. As if to confirm this, when
George decides to adopt a Christian attitude and bring about a
reconciliation with Robert, he is free from the troublesome
apparition until, having failed to carry out his aim, he begins instead 'to indulge in a little more liberty' (P: 60, O: 38).

The walk to Arthur's Seat is like a dream journey (P: 61;
O: 39). George is cloaked in the haze but finds the air sweet.
The trance-like passage is heavy with imagery: 'blue haze',
'dense smoke', 'delicious' air, the grass and flowers 'loaden with
dew'. George's senses are heightened and he cannot bear to
destroy the natural beauty of the cobweb shimmering with dew
on his hat. This lifts his spirits and prepares him for the vision
of the morning light diffusing through the haze into a rainbow
and 'halo of glory' (P: 62; O: 40). George seems to be in a state
of grace and so it comes as a double shock to him and the reader
when he is confronted by the image of Robert distorted on the
cloud. We may argue that, because George is in communion
with nature, it has effectively given him the warning that enables
him to save his life. At any rate the change of tone is dramatic.

The lyrical tone of the walk gives way to the panic of the ghastly cloud vision and then we are literally brought down to earth as George tumbles over Robert. The Editor continues this downward process by again presenting Robert in as disgusting and cowardly a light as possible, sneering that his nose seems automatically to bleed at the mere presence of any threat to himself. George is shown in a relatively good light as he is the pursued rather than the pursuer and he does eventually offer Robert the hand of friendship.

The incidents on Arthur's Seat also become a court issue. Like the riot at the Black Bull, the events become inextricably bound up in party influence and intrigue. The case is tried twice and each time the story is presented with a slightly different emphasis, according to the politcal affiliations of the judge. The outcome of the trial is that George is vindicated by the evidence of the guards at Queensberry-house who saw Robert go on to the hill after George. Events are quickly brought to a head when George is found dead outside a brothel after a riotous evening spent drinking with his Jacobite friends. This sordid end to his life contrasts sharply with the sensitive picture set up by the walk to Arthur's Seat. George has won our sympathy and his death is a tragic waste and a severe blow to his father, but how much of our sympathy has been engineered by the Editor? 'Sensitivity' is the more attractive way to interpret a sensuous, passionate character and events show that George *can* be hotheaded, quarrelling not only with Robert but also with his friend Drummond. On the other hand, George does inspire the loyal friendship of Adam Gordon and perhaps the worst we can say of him is that he is impetuous and young. We should ask ourselves now if the Editor's idea of 'gentility in deportment' (P: 44; O: 19) simply means that George is outwardly more presentable that Robert. What does George actually do that is kind and good, and how far has he earned the Editor's support largely because he comes from the right social class? In this book more than any other, we must always be conscious that appearances may be deceptive. But what are we to judge by — people's acts or their intentions?

Arabella Logan and Bell Calvert seek the murderer

The *Confessions* grips our attention because it moves so briskly along and includes several types of book all in one. After the comic history and caricature characters of the Colwan marriage, we have the high drama of the archetypal struggle between rival brothers. The next part of the Editor's Narrative is very like a detective story, with two new characters leading the action.

The laird dies convinced that the Wringhim household have caused George's death, leaving Arabella to unravel the mystery. The vulnerability of the individual and the difficulty of weighing actions against reasons is examined when Mrs Logan realises she must not judge Bell Calvert too severely or she will lose her assistance. Bell's trial makes similar points humorously through the pert manner and down-to-earth broad Scots answers of the maid Bessy Gillies. Her answers sometimes seem off-hand but are usually quite precise and based on sound commonsense although they can be bawdy and, like Gil-Martin, her aim is to obscure matters. Significantly she reminds us it is impossible to swear that what we believe is the objective truth. It is as well to bear this in mind when comparing the Editor's Narrative with Robert's Memoir.

Hogg plants numerous supernatural references throughout Bell Calvert's apparently straightforward account of events. Bell says that on the night of the murder she was where the devil intended her to be (P: 80; O: 61), suggesting that events were carefully manipulated by some evil force. Evil is also represented by Ridsley, whom Bell consistently describes as 'a lordly fiend' (P: 78; O: 59) and 'diabolical' (P: 96; O: 80). (A further reference to 'an artful and consummate fiend' (P: 87; O: 70) is to a previous man-friend who abandoned her in York.) On the surface, these references simply demonstrate Bell's extreme distress and her anger at associates who have betrayed her but it is part of the subtle effect of the book that so many words and phrases that seem to arise perfectly naturally and innocently from particular circumstances serve to develop the themes of the text as a whole. Ridsley plays a key role in witnessing the crime and in identifying Robert at the end of the Editor's Narrative — even though this contributes to the delay in sending officers to arrest him. He also 'tests' Bell who, like George and Mrs Logan earlier in the book, must choose between conflicting impulses. Her need for money prevents her from rejecting Ridsley and brings her further suffering and indignity. These tests of principle provide important yardsticks by which to measure Robert's actions later.

Ridsley is like the mysterious, anonymous figures, noted earlier, who appear at significant moments to drive on the a action. They prepare the way for Gil-Martin's shape-changing and these references remind us of the sudden disappearance of Robert's 'friend' on Arthur's Seat — a friend whom George at once identifies as the devil (P: 65; O: 44).

Supernatural involvement is also implied in Bell's description of George's death. She feels she is looking on a demon when she sees the figure in tartans and she has another presentiment of evil when Ridsley bursts into her room after Drummond leaves. These references to evil prepare us for the introduction of Gil-Martin and, since Bell seems reliable, her evidence seems to prove his existence and identify him with the devil. His actions all confirm that link since he is mysteriously aware of her presence but unafraid (he even winks at her); he shouts that hell has it when Robert moves to stab his brother and laughs exultantly after the event.

These events are echoed when the two women go to look for Robert near Dalcastle. Robert's companion again winks at Bell, confirming that they have met before, but this time he looks like the dead George, so that for the first time we may suspect that we are dealing with a supernatural shape-changer. However, it is Mrs Logan who 'recognises' the apparition as George and she immediately becomes hysterical. It may be that each of the women has seen what she wanted to see and that, on the murder night, Bell Calvert saw a figure looking like Thomas Drummond because she longed for him to return. Now she does not immediately think of George but quickly agrees to the suggestion. The women are overwrought and their 'heated imaginations' (P: 98; O: 83) seem to create a shared hysteria.

Once again Hogg, or his ironically superior Editor, undercuts the situation with humour and contrasts the 'fire' and 'flame' that 'gleamed from each' in their 'heated' condition with a picture of two dumb, grotesque gargoyles, 'with their hands spread, their eyes fixed, and their chops fallen down upon their bosoms' (P: 98; O: 83). The picture becomes even more absurd when the landlady joins in without knowing what she is speaking about. Her involvement — another chance interruption by an outsider — seems to confirm that the two women have let their imaginations overturn their reason. Nevertheless, it also brings Bell Calvert to see the absurdity of the situation. The women are left with the problem of comprehending the situation, since it now appears to them as if George is alive yet they both saw him dead.

Earlier, Bell had stressed that 'we have nothing on earth but our senses to depend upon' (P: 95; O: 80). Now she appeals to reason, suggesting that their 'disturbed imaginations' have conjured up a 'phantasy'. Mrs Logan reaffirms the power of the senses, adding 'Whose word, or whose reasoning can convince us against our own senses?' (P: 99; O: 85). The problem is that everyone may see the same things slightly differently (try getting people to agree on the same names for certain shades of colour!). Since no-one can share our exact perspective — no-one can see through our eyes — it means that the indivudual is frighteningly alone in the universe. We all have to trust that things are as we perceive them to be. The episode establishes these important points before moving on to Robert's Memoir which gives us the opportunity to view events through the eyes of someone with different experience, different preoccupations from our own.

This section also mentions Gil-Martin's name for the first time. This mysterious figure seems in control of the whole scene as he manipulates events to make all the other players suffer the maximum indignity. There is plenty of crude humour and dramatic irony as the two women, their disguise apparently useless, are forced to squat in the brambles, while Gil-Martin parades Robert in front of them and taunts them by urging Robert to describe the punishments he would inflict on them. Gil-Martin then abandons them to their scuffle, with Robert, a screaming black spider of a figure, easily 'mastered' by the two women. Robert is described as a repulsive fiend but he is clearly little more than Gil-Martin's tormented puppet: 'his flesh seems fading from his bones, as if the worm that never dies were gnawing it away already' (P: 104; O: 90).

The key to these last scenes lies in Robert's discussion with Gil-Martin who is clearly egging Robert on to some action, 'the other meritorious deed' (P: 101, O: 87). In order to persuade him, Gil-Martin reminds him of absolute predestination — the belief that God has planned every single human action so that, as Lady Dalcastle said, 'a justified person can do no wrong' (P: 39; O: 13). Robert is not sure. Ironically, he denies 'the boundlessness of the true Christian's freedom' (P: 100; O: 86), interpreting Christian freedom as the ability to break the commonly held moral laws. His argument, obsessed with sin, has perversely blinded him to the argument he *should* be using against Gil-Martin — that God gave human beings the power of Free Will to choose between good and evil, right and wrong. He is misinterpreting the idea of Christian 'freedom' and faulty reasoning has inverted his sense of right and wrong, leading him to commit an 'unnatural' crime — the murder of a brother. Like characters earlier in the book, Robert is facing choices but he is making the wrong decisions.

ROBERT'S MEMOIR

Plot Summary

Robert describes his early life, his skill in theology and his fear of ever-increasing sin. He has the beadle, John Barnet, dismissed for hinting that he is Robert Wringhim's son and defeats his school rival, M'Gill, by deception. On the day he learns that he is one of the 'elect', Robert meets a strange youth whom he eventually takes to be Czar Peter of Russia. This 'prince', who says his name is Gil-Martin, persuades Robert to join in killing the 'moderate' preacher Blanchard but Robert's bullet is the only one to take effect. The 'great sovereign' then urges Robert to kill his brother George on Arthur's Seat. Despite a supernatural warning, Robert goes on to the hill where George discovers him accidentally. He finally kills George outside a brothel and becomes Laird of Dalcastle but finds that events are happening of which he has no recollection: he is supposed to have seduced a young girl, dispossessed her mother and hired a new servant. He concludes he must have a double, learns that the local people think he is possessed and grows to dread Gil-Martin. On the discovery of his mother's body, he flees Dalcastle to escape the accusation of murder. He works in a printing-house in Edinburgh. printing his life story, but leaves when rumours spread that the devil is assisting the work. Pursued, sometimes by demons and sometimes by the inexorable Gil-Martin, Robert flees from cottage to cottage in the Borders till, in despair, he agrees to a suicide pact with Gil-Martin.

Robert's childhood and upbringing

Robert's Memoir opens with a dramatic change in tone. The Editor's detachment vanishes, replaced by Robert's insistence on 'My life . . . ', 'My sorrows . . . ', 'My mother . . . ' (P: 109; O: 97). The Editor occasionally exploits religious vocabulary and phrasing to undercut his subject with irony, but the Memoir opens in a style that is intensely and overwhelmingly Biblical. Every line is loaded with alliteration, lists of paired nouns, parallel contrasting clauses and the rich images of gold and silver, blood and sacrifice.

He is deliberately emotive: his mother represents 'purity' in the face of Colwan 'corruption', but this leads to obvious but self-protective inconsistencies. Immediately after telling us that his mother spent only one night with her husband, he announces that he is the second son of the marriage. Can Robert's pride really have led him to believe that he is the product of some latter-day immaculate conception? He imagines he has a 'conspicuous' and important role in the world but admits, not once but twice, that he has been an outcast, fatherless and nameless. It is in an effort to compensate for having so much less than others that he seeks to outdo them in every way and to attract as much attention and admiration as he can. Thus, in the 'Ineffectual Calling' episode, Robert is anxious not only to show his wit by splitting the concept in two but also to condemn others. As the Memoir goes on to prove, he completely fails to heed the 'warnings, doctrines, and reproofs' that he says others ignore (P: 110; O: 99).

The insecurity that leads Robert into conceited show stems from his solitary life and the severe predestinarian beliefs taught him by Wringhim Senior. Even his incessant prayers count for nothing if he is not one of the saved. His sins seem to compound themselves — he makes vows then breaks them, one lie leads to another and ordinary human frailty seems to grow into an overwhelming sea of sins, each begetting others. (See P: 111-2, 118; O: 100, 107-8). While we should ask ourselves how well we measure up against the same strict standards, Robert's concern with sin seems to be inspired partly by fear of damnation and partly by a need to maintain external appearance and preserve a mask. (See Barnet's comment, P: 112; O: 101.) He regrets his sins when he remembers they will prevent his being saved but he admits to relishing the results of some of these same sins, for example, the deceptions which get M'Gill into trouble. In fact, Robert seems to swing between crippling anxiety and smug complacency as he compares himself to the heroes of the Old Testament (P: 118, O: 108).

We are likely to agree with John Barnet's assessment of Robert that he's 'a conceited gowk' (P: 111; O: 99). Since Robert's mother and his 'reverend father' inflate his impression of himself, Barnet serves as a useful objective standard for the reader, in the same way that Bell Calvert did in the previous section. As Wringhim's beadle he presumably shares a commitment to Presbyterian religious views and this should make it quite clear that Hogg has no intention of attacking religion itself. His targets are those people who distort religion to their own glorification, denying ordinary individuals the right to live by their own consciences.

Robert fears John Barnet because the beadle has seen through some of his 'notorious lies' (as usual, Robert presents an odd mixture of malice and honesty). While Robert reacts with Biblical oratory, Barnet, like the maid Bessy Gillies, brings things back down to a human level with some earthy Scots expressions. Barnet's language is concrete, direct and wholesome after Robert's grand phrases and he offers the breath of reality, the contact with daily life that seems so dismally lacking in the Wringhim household. He seems eminently sensible and his role as reliable commentator is enhanced by the proverbial folk wisdom that he uses — 'Gin the bannet fits . . . ' (P: 115; O: 104). Despite a low opinion of Robert, he wants to see fair play in the fight between M'Gill and Robert and holds that the ends do not justify the means: Robert may be bad but to resort to fighting him unfairly makes his opponent bad too. Straightforward and unpretentious as he is, Barnet can also match the Wringhims in scripture knowledge and is able to expose the vanity of the Reverend Mr Wringhim through a reference to the hypocrisy of the Pharisee in the temple. Like Bessy Gillies, he refuses to say what cannot be proved and, like Bell Calvert, he faces a choice between self-respect and material well-being. He chooses self-respect and refuses to let the minister tell him how to think.

Robert's encounter with M'Gill is equally instructive even though we depend almost entirely on Robert's assessment of his rival. The Editor told us that it was in school that Robert excelled yet even here his position is usurped. Faced with M'Gill's superior intellectual gifts, and finding himself cast down by comparison, Robert shows himself more than willing to believe in black magic and supernatural intervention: he decides that M'Gill's mother is a witch and that M'Gill himself is in league with the devil (P: 119; O: 109). Significantly, Robert brings about M'Gill's downfall by *imitating* his skills and creating *likenesses* of the teachers in absurd postures. The actions are like those of Gil-Martin while M'Gill, finding himself accused of things he cannot account for, foreshadows Robert's fate. When he is accused of cursing, M'Gill finds himself tongue-tied and inarticulate, just as Robert will be in the face of Gil-Martin's eloquence (P: 121; O: 111). This echo is mirrored by the similarity between the names of Robert's 'rival' and 'friend': M'Gill/Gil-Martin. One other comparison is worth making. Robert's short-lived triumph over M'Gill allows him to stand as 'king of the class' (P: 120; O: 110) giving him a little of the public attention that George basks in in Edinburgh as 'king of the game' on the tennis court (P: 46; O: 21).

His treatment of M'Gill exposes Robert as a sneak and a coward, ready to grovel in the face of any physical threat so, when he goes on to give his own complacent assessment of himself and his actions, it is difficult not to despise him. Unlike Barnet, he seems to think that any means justify an end since he does not regret lying to get the things he wants and smugly believes that even if M'Gill did not deserve punishment for the reason it was given to him, he probably deserved it for something anyway (P: 119; O: 109). Yet Robert does not apply these principles to himself — he thinks that the more he sins, the more welcome his salvation will be in heaven (P: 123; O: 114)! His list of self-confessed sins and his phobia about women (whom he sees as luring men towards sexual sins) make him appear at best ridiculous, at worst perverted and hypocritical.

Meeting Gil-Martin

The pace of the book is carefully handled so that, having formed an assessment about Robert from his treatment of Barnet and M'Gill, we are ready at last to encounter Gil-Martin properly. The consistent references to fiends and devils have set up an expectation of something dramatic but Gil-Martin's entry is subtle and insidious.

He appears at a key moment in Robert's life, the very day when the Reverend Mr Wringhim announces that Robert is one of those chosen by God for salvation (P: 124; O: 115). For Robert, this is a moment of rebirth: 'my whole frame seemed to be renewed; every nerve was buoyant with new life' (P: 125; O: 115-6) and it brings an end at last to the terrifying threat of everlasting damnation, since his 'reverend father' assures him that 'All the powers of darkness ... shall never be able to pluck you again out of your Redeemer's hand' (P: 124; O: 115). But Robert quickly gives way to exultant pride and, as he imagines himself soaring heavenwards like an eagle, contemptuously gazing on 'the grovelling creatures below', we should remember that pride was the sin that caused Satan to fall from grace (P: 125; O: 116).

This is the cue for Gil-Martin. Robert senses there is something unusual about the stranger but he ignores the warnings: 'I felt a sort of invisible power'; 'strange sensations thrilled through my whole frame', and later, 'an involuntary inclination to escape from his presence' (P: 125, 127; O: 116, 118). The signs would be instantly recognisable to someone familiar with folk tradition and would lend terrible irony to Gil-Martin's opening words of assurance that they share the same beliefs. Robert reports their conversation, obtusely blind to the real import of his companion's words, but the reader is delighted by all the clever double-talk and the subtle play on different word senses. Robert hears what he wants to hear — and so does the reader. Robert is just clever enough to fear that Gil-Martin's ideas might be blasphemous — we readers congratulate ourselves that we are not so foolish as Robert. But why is it that Robert is so anxious to see and hear the best in Gil-Martin?

Robert has never known any affectionate companionship and here he meets for the first time someone who expresses pleasure and 'deference' in meeting him (P: 127; O: 118). It would not be too strong to say that Robert becomes infatuated with Gil-Martin for he admits he cannot stay out of his company (P: 136; O: 128). Gil-Martin bombards Robert with ideas and keeps him on the move, literally and mentally, so that he becomes confused and ignores his original intention of praying. (Compare this with the consequences of George's failure to hold to good intentions, discussed earlier.)

The encounter changes Robert. His family recognises this and the reader can detect it in Robert's changed tone. He writes with confusion and uncertainty, dwelling on the date, which coincides with the feast of the Annunciation. (Gil-Martin's arrival is a black parody of the Angel Gabriel's visit to Mary, announcing that she is to bear Jesus.) His family's fear that Satan has been at work with Robert seems to confirm our interpretation of Gil-Martin and, when his mother suggests that the devil can take the form of an 'angel of light' (P: 129; O: 121), it may remind us that 'Lucifer', one of the many names for the devil, means 'light bearer'. Wringhim Senior, obsessed with hell as something black and sinister, — 'the kingdom of darkness' (P: 130 O: 121) — dismisses the idea but his distorted Biblical language is a clue that he is wrong.

Robert's confidence reasserts itself next day when his 'reverend father' dedicates him to the Lord. It is just as much a mark of Robert's lack of self-knowledge as of his pride and latent aggression that he sees himself as a soldier of the Church, a triumphant 'champion' and an avenging 'sword' to 'cut sinners off'. This 'macho' fantasy is the opposite of his real, cowardly character and the main reason he can contemplate these actions is that he sees 'sinners' as less than human, as some form of troublesome, rather distasteful vermin to be eradicated from earth (P: 130-31; O: 122-23).

His extreme state of pride makes Robert susceptible to Gil-Martin. He marvels at Gil-Martin's book 'all intersected with red lines, and verses', ignoring the physical shock it gives him and misunderstanding the significance of Gil-Martin's emphasis in 'It is *my* Bible'. The reader remembers that the names of those 'consigned to everlasting destruction' were 'written on the red-letter side of the book of life' (P: 114; O:102). If Gil-Martin is the devil, then he refers to his own damnation when he tells Robert that his shape-changing ability is 'a peculiarity in my nature, a gift of the God that made me; but whether or not given me for a blessing, he knows himself, and so do I' (P: 132; O: 125). Robert is seduced by the mildness, affability and modesty of his companion but these are only masks which Gil-Martin drops quickly so that Robert is soon the follower, not the leader.

This is a relief to Robert, just as it is is to know that he can stop pretending to be pure since Gil-Martin can read 'his most secret thoughts' (P: 133; O: 125). Indeed, far from being repelled by Robert's 'natural character', Gil-Martin says it is the very thing that attracts him to Robert. Step by step, Robert becomes 'captivated' by this 'fascinating' character till Gil-Martin dominates him completely, driving him, on occasion, to 'shed tears at being obliged to yield to proposals against which I had at first felt every reasoning power of my soul rise in opposition' (P: 135; O: 127). Their relationship allows Robert to indulge the extremes of his character — his need for flattery and attention and his masochistic pleasure in abasement.

Gil-Martin is suave, fluent and plausible, telling just enough of the truth to confuse the endlessly gullible Robert. Like the rational Editor of the first part, he presents apparently logical arguments selectively and persuasively to Robert who then suppresses his own intuitive reactions. Gil-Martin's skill lies in knowing Robert's willingness to be led. In any case, if Gil-Martin *is* Satan, then, by the laws of tradition, his conquest will be useless if Robert does not come of his own free will. Thus Gil-Martin never lies but, conversely, never explains completely. For example, when he says 'Gil' is not his *Christian* name and 'proudly' announces that he has 'no parents save one, whom I do not acknowledge' (P: 136; O: 129), Robert is satisfied but the reader is alerted. 'Gil-Moules' is one of the names for the devil in Scottish mythology (James Hogg uses it himself in other works) and 'Gille Mairtean the fox' is a shape-changing supernatural helper in Highland folklore. In Christian belief, evil is personified by Satan, who was God's brightest and best angel until excessive pride caused him to attempt to become God himself, for which he and his followers were cast out from heaven into eternal suffering in hell. Robert does not even understand the full significance of his own words when he says that no man was ever created like his 'patron' — for in Christian belief mankind, unlike devils or angels, was created in the image of God. Gil-Martin alerts us to the theme of hypocrisy when he says that all his subjects believe that they are Christians (P: 142; O: 136) but Robert's own complacent pride does not allow him to see the danger he is in and he assumes his friend is Czar Peter of Russia in disguise.

The murder of Blanchard‧

In their conversations, Gil-Martin continually tests Robert to see what extreme viewpoints he will hold, what basic moral laws he will break. He is leading Robert in small steps to the point where he can contemplate and perhaps at last undertake the serious crimes that will condemn him to hell. The first major test is the murder of the moderate Presbyterian minister, Blanchard, whose goodness is signalled by the fact that Gil-Martin does not like him and is forced to leave when he is present. Blanchard recognises the flaw in Gil-Martin's arguments — that they are extreme and driven by fear rather than Christian love. He describes religion as a positive bond in society, something that unites people in co-operation and mutual support (P: 138; O: 131), thus expressing eloquent criticism of the Wringhim view, which is self-absorbed and divides humanity into 'them' and 'us', regardless even of natural bonds of family, kinship and community. He warns Robert that the Bible can be quoted to prove any argument good or bad and cautions him that extending the extreme ideas of absolute predestination is leading him to 'damnation'. He almost persuades Robert to give up Gil-Martin, showing that Robert is not completely lost but also that he has almost no convictions of his own — his is a suggestible mind to be won and led by whichever voice is loudest at the moment.

Compared with Blanchard, Gil-Martin appears sullen and petulant, gradually exerting more power over Robert but also beginning to show contempt for him. He warns Robert that he is more than a mortal man, advising him to reconsider the matter when Robert still cannot understand (P: 139; O: 133). Robert,

however, cannot see the simple answer. He ignores the unambig-
uous commandment 'Thou shalt not kill', preferring Gil-Martin's
sophistry which says that it will be all right to kill Blanchard
because either it is a service to humanity or, if he is a good man,
he will go to heaven. He allows 'logical' conundrums to drive
out simple sense. He becomes possessed by Gil-Martin's ideas,
dreaming about them, and allowing them to distort his understanding. Blanchard's sermon, which preaches that everyone can
be saved, challenges the idea of predestination and seems to
threaten Robert's guaranteed salvation.

The murder of Blanchard is a sinful act of such magnitude
that it calls up more than the usual warning portents. Robert
feels a veil drawn over him as he looks to heaven for support
(P: 143; O: 137); he sees golden weapons all pointing menacingly
at him (P: 144; O: 138). Gil-Martin's violent reaction suggests
that the visions are heavenly warnings although Robert interprets them as signs to continue. Gil-Martin encourages this by
presenting him with guns like those in the vision. Once again the
pace and tone of the writing reflect Robert's vacillating mind
and changing emotions. He rushes eagerly towards Gil-Martin
and the proposed crime but, as Blanchard approaches, time
slows down: 'Blanchard [was] . . . coming slowly', 'He came
deliberately on . . . ', 'he . . . came onward', 'approaching
step by step'. Blanchard's innocent 'swinging air', his 'ease and
indifference' are contrasted with Robert's agonised cry that the
scene will live with him 'either in the narrow bounds of time or
the ages of eternity' (P: 145; O: 139-40).

Robert is given a last chance to repent by the 'sweet voice'
that whispers beware. We do not know if it is a sign of heavenly
intervention or the voice of Robert's conscience because Gil-
Martin taunts him as a coward. Naturally, Gil-Martin's bullet
cannot affect Blanchard for either Gil-Martin is the product of
Robert's inflamed imagination or, if he is the devil incarnate,
then he can have no power over the innocent clergyman who,
even as he dies pathetically scrabbling at the earth, is so full of
genuine Christian spirit and dignity that his last words are a
prayer for forgiveness. The murder is a turning point for, like
Robert's lies of old, it leads directly to the death of another
man, the young preacher who is hanged for the murder. It also
proves the fallibility of the law courts and the need to wait for
divine justice to punish the crime.

Contempt for the legal system leads Robert to plot to kid-
nap the leaders of the rival political/religious party. This curious

incident, like most of the events of Robert's early life, is unknown to the Editor. The plot fails and, since Robert is forced like George to 'walk circumspectly' and be more careful, he consequently sees less of Gil-Martin. They arrange a password, rather as witches in covens have a magic word to call on the devil. Robert's holy war has led to secrecy, not triumph.

In the meantime, growing evidence suggests that Gil-Martin is a supernatural agent of evil. He never stays in one place and emerges as increasingly haughty and imperious: his crusade is for 'the advancement of my own power and dominion, or . . . thwarting my enemies' (P: 149; O: 144). His flattery of Robert is clearly exposed as a device to lead Robert to another test: will he murder his own brother? Now, instead of using only the distorted arguments of religious debate, Gil-Martin appeals to Robert's greed by reminding him the Dalcastle estates will become his. This indicates the further debasement of Robert's character but Robert does not succumb immediately and he voices his doubts and uncertainties so that we begin to share his sense of confusion. It may not be enough for him to say, like some war criminal, 'I was prompted, by one who knew right and wrong much better than I did' (P: 151; O: 146-7), or to say that constantly thinking about it made the deed seem easier but we must at least feel sorry for this weak, buffeted spirit and understand, without necessarily condoning, the reasons for his envy and hatred of the Colwans and his desperate need to believe he is one of the chosen people.

Robert's account of the meetings with George and his death

Ignoring the ambiguity of Gil-Martin's promise that he will become 'a master spirit of desolation in the dwellings of the wicked' (P: 152; O: 148), Robert is eager to confront George. Remember that George seems to have the advantage over Robert in every way: his name and parentage are acknowledged, when rejected by his mother he is immediately claimed by the laird; he is apparently personable and good-looking; is wealthy, enjoys a good social position and has numerous friends. It is hardly surprising that Robert resents him and clings to his supposed spiritual superiority to balance the scales. Robert convinces himself that George is wallowing in 'a sink of sin' (P: 152; O: 148) but it is when George 'proves' his iniquity by swearing (remember Psalm 109 above) that Robert feels justified to act. When George hits back, Robert suffers another sinful passion, anger, 'the choler that is always inspired by the wicked one', the very passion of which he first accuses George (P: 153; O: 148). By now he is intent on George's destruction.

At this point Robert is conveyed to prison and the worldly-wise jailer brings a refreshing change of pace and an opportunity for humour to add to the irony in Gil-Martin's double-edged speeches and our incredulous laughter at Robert's naivety throughout the Memoir. The jailer reminds us that the world is indeed a pretty corrupt place: prisoners need influential friends to plead their cases and the jailer is disappointed that his prisoner is not a wealthy source of tips. For him Robert is just another noisy 'praying prisoner', more trouble than he is worth, as in the old days of the Covenanting Wars. Nevertheless, the jailer offers some refreshing commonsense, blowing away the atmosphere of hellfire and jealousy when he treats Robert's supposed mission to slay him as a joke and a sign that Robert is a bit crazy but essentially harmless (P: 154; O: 150).

Any lingering doubts Robert has about the wickedness of the Colwans and the morality of killing George are dealt a severe knock by the Reverend Mr Wringhim's prayers 'making it plain to all my senses of perception, that they were beings given up of God' (P: 155; O: 151). As Bell Calvert warns, once our senses deceive us, we have no guide or protection. To Robert the subsequent trial is like some triumph in a holy war — his foes scatter before him like the sea parting for Moses but the breakdown of his senses manifests itself in yet another way. He experiences a 'strange distemper', imagining himself 'to be two people' (one Gil-Martin, one George) and he always sees one on his left side (the mirror-image of the curse in the psalm *and* of the apparition George experiences) (P: 157; O: 153-4). Robert's personality, formerly showing cracks, now starts to crumble under the intensity of his own passions and the contradictions in his character. He blames witchcraft, as he did when M'Gill mortified him, and once again he blames a woman: 'my father's reputed concubine'. Though Robert means Arabella Logan, the phrase could equally well mean his mother and fits in with the latent dislike of her that he has already mentioned on two occasions (P: 128, 136; O: 120, 128-9). Robert also notes with distress that he was accused wrongly of pursuing his brother at this time (the period when George was haunted by Robert's image with unnaturally fierce eyes). Robert guesses that Gil-Martin's shape-changing is to blame and their relationship changes.

Robert now flatters Gil-Martin ('great prince') and stresses his willingness to take part in all his 'future operations' while

Gil-Martin becomes openly contemptuous of Robert's empty phrases: 'You are free of your words and your promises' (P: 159; O: 156). Gil-Martin leads Robert to Arthur's Seat, promising him he can easily despatch George and giving him a knife. Robert's version fits with the Editor's Narrative in that he asks the guards if George has gone on to the hill (he can't believe that someone so wicked gets up so early in the morning!). Alone, at St Anthony's Well, he is beset by doubts, aware that 'by the laws of men' his crimes are serious. In this state of doubt, he hears a 'still small voice' similar to the one he heard before Blanchard's murder. (When the prophet Elijah is dejected because his efforts seem to be coming to nothing, the Lord speaks to him as 'a still small voice' bidding him return to Damascus to his work — 1 Kings 19: 12.) Robert also sees 'a lady, robed in white', an image suggestive of purity. (In folklore, wells often have supernatural guardians.) This spirit rebukes him and bids him go home and, in confusion, he is almost ready to obey. Gil-Martin's response to this apparition is as hostile as it was to the others: he distorts the woman's words and describes her as a 'wench', a word whose derogatory overtones must appeal to Robert's obsessive feelings that women are corrupt.

Gil-Martin plays on Robert's fear, leading him to feel guilty then urging him on by promising to divert George's attention (the distorted vision of Robert). He shows 'a certain derisive exultation of expression' (P: 162; O: 160) when Robert denies he wants the Dalcastle money out of greed. As at Blanchard's death, Robert is gripped by powerful images, this time of George hurtling to his death; the jagged rocks; George's screams. His troubled mind also generates the less worthy thought that he may fall over himself and become the victim. The result is that Robert cannot do the deed, either through cowardice or because he still has lingering scruples and we should remember John Barnet when Robert says, 'These THOUGHTS are hard enemies wherewith to combat!' (P: 164; O: 161). Barnet relates thoughts to principles, saying he will 'aye be master o' his ain thoughts' (P: 117; O: 107); Robert's problem is that he is bombarded by conflicting thoughts and cannot hold to a sensible, organising principle that will show him which to follow and which to reject. His crippling inability to direct his actions results in an emotional outburst as he weeps in frustration because he cannot push George. Ultimately it is fear of Gil-Martin's wrath that prompts Robert to rise when, as a Christian, fear of God's judgement should have prevented him. Robert's fear of

Gil-Martin is slowly growing to be his strongest, most durable emotion.

Robert's hypocrisy is also growing. He notes contentedly his father's anger at the sight of 'me bleeding a second time by the hand of a brother' (P: 164; O: 162), regardless of the fact that he sought out George to kill him. At the trial he also claims that George lies but that his own evidence 'was not the truth' (P: 165; O: 163). This was by the advice of both Wringhim Senior and Gil-Martin, two characters whose views seem to accord particularly well. When George is acquitted at the second trial, Robert condemns the judge as wicked and rejoices when Gil-Martin engineers his death. The first judge, who supports the Wringhim cause, strikes him as 'just and righteous', able to do what Robert cannot: 'discern between a righteous and a wicked man' (P: 165; O: 163).

Gil-Martin offers Robert a 'bond of blood' (P: 167; O: 165) that he will never be harmed by *human* hand and so the scene is set for the final attack on George, with Gil-Martin leaving Robert to the agony of his own confused thoughts, 'a thing my friend never failed in subjecting me to' (P: 169; O: 167). To encourage himself, Robert sings part of the 10th Psalm, which includes lines that apply equally as well to Robert as to the supposed wickedness of his victim:

> The wicked of his heart's desire
>   doth talk with boasting great;
> He blesseth him that's covetous,
>   whom yet the Lord doth hate.
> The wicked, through his pride of face,
>   on God he doth not call;
> And in the counsels of his heart
>   the Lord is not at all.

Robert resists Gil-Martin's insistent promptings as long as he can till Gil-Martin applies the emotional blackmail that *he* will do the deed, implying that, as his safety has not been secured, he may perish. Gil-Martin's contempt is too much for Robert, who says he 'had no life' except with Gil-Martin's approval. His need for Gil-Martin even over-rides the 'chilling vibrations' he experiences on seeing Gil-Martin's transformation into a High-lander (P: 170; O: 169). Distraught, suffering both 'vexation' and 'despair', Robert remembers little of the fight except that George came out 'urging a reconciliation, as was his wont on such occasions' (P: 171; O: 170). George, 'firm as a rock', belongs to the natural world, while his adversary belongs to the element of air, flitting 'like a shadow, or rather like a spirit'. After the murder, Robert tries to believe he acted honourably, suggesting he ran to Gil-Martin's aid. He is forced to deny his own senses to accept Gil-Martin's version that he fought valiantly and that George died cursing. Robert's only defence for his actions lies in his customary arguments that it was done for a higher cause and that the Bible shows that 'the final extinction of the wicked and profane' is acceptable (P: 172; O: 172).

This contradiction and the fear of discovery causes Robert's second breakdown. Gil-Martin is exultant at achieving Robert's mortal crime but immediately suggests killing the laird so that Robert has no peace. Despite these macabre scenes there is room for black humour when Robert reports his relief and Gil-Martin's frustration that the laird dies before he can be murdered. Robert later tries to make amends by offering to despatch Mrs Logan (P: 173-4; O: 173). Like an unhappy lover, Robert tries to enjoy their 'success' for the sake of Gil-Martin, marvelling when Drummond is accused of George's death as it seems that heaven really does favour Robert. He admits that it was beyond his 'comprehension', that he could not 'perceive' what gain the church made by these deeds (P: 173; O: 173).

Gradual breakdown

Once installed as laird, Robert says Gil-Martin thwarts his good intentions. Robert's confusion grows as mounting contradictions beset him. On the one hand, he restates his obsessive fear of sexual compromise through 'private confabulations with women' (P: 174; O: 174). (The mystery of his own birth and the repressive teachings of the Reverend Mr Wringhim must go a long way to explaining this prejudice.) On the other hand he finds himself accused of sexually exploiting a girl and of causing legal documents to be forged in order to acquire both the family land and the compliance of the girl involved. He finds once more that the passage of time has become distorted and that he is believed to be a habitual drunk (though he remembers taking alcohol only once). Worst of all, he finds that Gil-Martin sides with his accusers and taunts him by appearing as George.

Hogg relieves the tension with humour directed at the talkative lawyer, who is too insensitively preoccupied with money

and the letter of the law to worry about supernatural spirits —
or justice. Again Hogg attacks corruption in the legal system and
at the same time hugely enjoys the linguistic fireworks of the
writ, where he piles on old Scots words and legal terms.

Robert is meantime forced to account for all the contradictions and reaches two possible conclusions: either he has a
double or his personality is literally disintegrating so that he is
possessed by some other spirit (P: 181; O: 182). This is a key
stage, where Robert gives way to terror, panic and a knowledge
that he is frightened and oppressed by Gil-Martin. He longs for
'utter oblivion' to resolve the chaos and sublimates his anger for
Gil-Martin by transferring it to his mother, whom he now finds
'exceedingly obnoxious' (P: 183; O: 184).

After taking refuge for a second time in drink, he finds
there has been another apparent time leap. Six months have
seemingly passed and he finds he has a new servant and garish
clothes. Gil-Martin has gone off with Wringhim Senior, since
their views are so compatible, and Robert's mother has dis-
appeared. These last two items bring Robert a short-lived sense
of relief till Gil-Martin arrives in the shape of George, his appearance and voice assaulting Robert's senses (P: 186-7; O: 188).
Robert now finds Gil-Martin's presence loathsome and repellent
and he cringes as Gil-Martin now adopts a nagging, insistent
tone, ominously telling Robert that they are indivisible and that
'never shall I depart from this country until I can carry you in
triumph with me' (P: 187; O: 189). He continues his attack on
Robert using words like 'sunk', 'falling off' and 'debasement'
that illustrate Robert's humiliation and contrast sharply with
the earlier phrases like 'high' and 'exalted' (P: 188; O: 190).
He becomes Robert's accuser, telling him he has murdered both
his mother and the girl he seduced and Robert comes to feel
that he is in the coils of a serpent (think of the Garden of Eden),
a serpent that is toying with him but is not yet ready to despatch him.

But Hogg is not yet ready for the grand finale. He introduces
an episode where Robert is contrasted with another represent-
ative of common humanity, Samuel Scrape. As a Cameronian,
Scrape is a follower of one of the severest Presbyterian sects,
one that broke away from the established Church of Scotland
because it was not strict enough. Nevertheless, Scrape does not
have an over-idealised view of human aspirations. His story
about the Cameronian accepting double payment for the cow
illustrates more hypocrisy but also shows that it is against

human nature to look a gift horse in the mouth and that you will find a certain measure of self-interest in any walk of life. It seems too that he is not above gossiping and he tells Robert that the common folk think he is in league with the devil. Finally he repeats the fable of the Auchtermuchty Sermon as a lesson that hypocrisy and corruption abound in even the most sanctified walks of life. Like Blanchard he warns that the devil can use the Bible 'to answer his ain ends' (P: 193; O: 196).

Events at Dalcastle draw to a close with the appearance of Arabella Logan and Bell Calvert, as described in the Editor's Narrative, and the discoveries of the bodies of Robert's mother and the seduced girl, Gil-Martin being the agent of discovery in all cases. Robert's self-loathing makes him wish to be less than human, a 'worm' or 'moth', to be 'crushed' as he had formerly wished to extinguish sinners. The cottagers reassert the idea that the supernatural is also an agent of divine justice when they want Robert to touch the body of his mother since it is a traditional belief that bodies will bleed again if touched by their murderer.

Robert's flight

Robert begins an erratic, troubled journey, running away from his crimes, Gil-Martin and even himself, aware now that he has wasted his education and his ambitions and that people see him as 'a monster of nature'. Gil-Martin's effect on Robert is symbolically suggested when Robert finds that wearing Gil-Martin's clothes releases evil thoughts (P: 204; O: 209).

His first stop is at a weaver's cottage where John Dods and his family reluctantly agree to give Robert lodgings. The cottagers represent both charity and a healthy respect for the supernatural when they give Robert shelter but them confine him in a small room with the weaver's loom. Robert becomes entangled in the loom in much the same way as he has been entangled by his own ideas and by Gil-Martin's machinations (P: 209-10; O: 215). The weaver's dream that Robert is the devil and the mysterious disappearance of Gil-Martin's knife and clothes force Robert onward.

In Edinburgh, Robert's education enables him to find work in a printing house. Hogg had been at the mercy of printers often enough when getting his own work published. (His negotiations with printers usually involved haggling over money and then being told that his work was too risqué for contemporary moral taste.) He clearly enjoyed getting his own back by making jokes concerning the printing trade and, since printers' assistants used to be called printers' devils, Robert seems to have come to the right place. He grows more confident and regains some of his old hypocritical haughtiness, dismissing his new friend Linton as 'a flippant unstable being' (P: 213; O: 220). He persuades the printer, a busy, self-important man who adopts a sanctimonious high moral tone, that the memoir is 'a religious parable' (P: 214; O: 221) but the interlude quickly ends when Gil-Martin, described by the printers as 'the devil', is seen assisting the printing. Robert is again reduced to despair and to flight, running blindly from Gil-Martin.

The rest of the Memoir is supposed to be a hand-written diary. Robert heads south towards the Border country longing now for the wings of a dove, the bird of peace, rather than those of the proud eagle, as in the past. (See also Psalm 55, verse 6, where the psalmist longs for the wings of a dove in order to fly to a place of rest.) However, Robert's tortured spirit can find no rest for he wakes in the stable at Dalkeith to hear a voice he recognises (Gil-Martin's) and he immediately contemplates suicide. At this stage he realises suicide is a crime against God's law and immediately begs forgiveness (P: 217; O: 224). Two beings now appear to argue over who shall have Robert and the uneasiness of the animals is a sign of some evil presence. Robert takes refuge with the animals and once again stumbles round in the dark, the confusion among the horses mirroring his moral blindness.

As he becomes progressively more lame and mutilated, he tries to believe that his is a moral pilgrimage but his body and soul seem more and more in conflict (P: 219; O: 227). This makes it easy for Gil-Martin to encourage his despair by reminding him that they are united. Robert sees Gil-Martin's exultation but is still unable to reject the idea that he is elect, so cannot completely reject Gil-Martin who seems inextricably bound up with this belief (P: 221; O: 229-30).

Robert still feels superior to the Douglas family at the inn in Ancrum and the Reverend Mr Wringhim would certainly disapprove of the fact that they were often too busy working to find time to pray as a family but, as Samuel Scrape reminded us, there are times when even the most God-fearing put day-to-day survival first. They still respect religion and their honest simplicity is a welcome contrast to Robert's pretensions. Their suspicion of an Oxford education and 'theology', which they think is the same as the 'black arts' of witchcraft and

satanism (P: 222; O: 230), is one in the eye for Edinburgh sophis-
ticates such as the Editor, who might be inclined to look down
on the simple Border folk. Robert hears the same debate about
who is to have him and, when he is cast out into the night, he is
attacked by the 'crimson paws' of fiends (P: 224; O: 233) who
seem to be controlled by Gil-Martin. Robert is more and more
driven to the desperate idea that suicide is his only escape, a
course which Gil-Martin is eager to encourage. By sinking into
despair and denying God's existence through failing either to
appeal to him or to have faith in him, Robert's suicide will de-
liver him, by his own hand, to hell. Robert ignores this for,
when he looks on Gil-Martin, he finds that, just as the Reverend
Mr Wringhim's psalm prophesied, his 'spirit, blood, and bones,
were all withered at the blasting sight' (P: 225; O: 235). Robert
hopes that suicide will prevent further torment from Gil-Martin
and from his own thoughts.

The diary now becomes increasingly hurried and disjointed,
using the present tense to add urgency and immediacy. Robert
finds some peace and more kindness among simple shepherds
although his presence provokes a disagreement. The shepherds
believe the traditional ideas about the supernatural while their
master adopts the educated, rational approach and 'mocks at
the idea of supernatural agency' (P: 227; O: 237). Ironically,
Robert's unsettling presence makes the master begin to doubt
his views. Meantime Robert, deprived of rest and sleep, is under-
going mental and physical disintegration so he eventually uses
Gil-Martin's short 'ejaculatory prayer' with an underlying
meaning that Robert senses is blasphemous (P: 228; O: 238).
Tragically, he guesses that he may be damned but his fear drives
him to suicide: 'My hour is at hand. — Almighty God, what is
this that I am about to do! The hour of repentance is past, and
now my fate is inevitable' (P: 230; O: 240).

THE EDITOR'S NARRATIVE (2)

Plot summary

The Editor prints a letter describing the discovery of a suicide's grave in the Borders. The Editor and some friends locate the grave, with the help of a shepherd. They disinter the body and discover Robert's Memoir. The Editor admits he is confused about whether the story is true and suggests Robert imagined Gil-Martin in his madness.

The discovery of the body and the Editor's summing up

The Editor reprints a letter from James Hogg to *Blackwood's Magazine*. This satisfies our curiosity by giving us an idea how Robert died but it also prompts questions about the authenticity of Robert's version. According to the letter, the youth who committed suicide 'had been a considerable time in the place' (P: 231 O: 241) and he seems to have stolen goods from the house. We may begin to wonder who is right since not all the circumstantial details tally. Tradition says the events took place one hundred and five years previously, that is in 1718, not 1712 as Robert's diary says. The Hogg of the letter does admit that some people say it might have been earlier. There are two descriptions of opening the grave which would be especially dramatic for readers in Edinburgh in the 1820s, as it was the time of the bodysnatchers and 'resurrectionists'.

Hogg adds to the confusion over what is reality by introducing some of his own acquaintances, including John Lockhart, who casts doubt on Hogg's reliability (P: 235, O: 246). Lockhart, like John Wilson (another of Hogg's literary friends), was educated at Glasgow University and Oxford and the Editor identifies himself with this highly privileged circle. Hogg further blurs the distinctions between the real and fictional worlds by introducing himself as a character who carefully dissociates himself from the grave-robbing and appears in the same down-to-earth light as John Dods and Tam Douglas, who were suspicious of Robert. He deliberately undermines his own letter by having another shepherd disagree with all the details of it.

After the two separate exhumations of the body, complete with lurid details, it comes as a relief when the Editor tries to restore calm and reason. Yet even he admits himself puzzled for, as a member of 'the present generation', brought up to believe in a rational world, he cannot accept 'that a man should be daily tempted by the devil, in the semblance of a fellow-creature' (P: 242; O: 254). His psychological interpretation offers the 'modern' mind a chance to dismiss the power of the supernatural but it cannot completely dispel his disturbed sense of confusion.

CONCLUSION

The novel appeared in 1824, following the diappointing reception of *The Three Perils of Man* and *The Three Perils of Woman*. Hogg had recently run into financial difficulties over a farming venture, besides which he had to support a young family and his wife's parents. Looking back on the time, he said, 'I was all this while writing as if in desperation', adding of the *Confessions*: 'it being a story replete with horror, after I had written it I durst not venture to put my name to it: so it was published anonymously, and of course did not sell very well'.[5] Despite the early lack of sales, the book is a very successful one, widely regarded as a masterpiece due to its careful structure and psychological insight.

The book as parable

When we finish the book, we may find ourselves in the same confused state as the Editor. The story may be, as both he and Robert suggest, a religious parable like *A Pilgrim's Progress*. There is a careful matching of characters: distorted, self-righteous characters on one side (Reverend Mr Wringhim, Lady Dalcastle, Robert); sincere, well-intentioned characters on the other (Blanchard, Barnet, the Border cottagers). The parable is a triumph of open-minded moderation since it presents positively characters who, by conventional moral codes, should be seen as flawed or suspect. Bell Calvert is held to be a thief and a prostitute; it seems probable Arabella Logan is the laird's mistress; the laird himself represents an easy-going sort of morality; George drinks, brawls and consorts with prostitutes. None of these characters can be held up as a pure, moral example but each clearly demands our sympathy and our support. They remind us that real people are flawed and occasionally need to have allowances made for them. Hogg's targets are those who set themselves up above others; those who assume that only they are right; those who use their influence or status to bolster their own position and intimidate others. His main examples are Robert and the Reverend Mr Wringhim but the Editor, who seems reliable, can also be opinionated and patronising.

It is important to remember that the book is not an attack on religion or any one branch of religion. Hogg shows in this and other books that he admires sincere religious faith: what he detests in the Wringhims is their lack of sincerity and their ability to warp religious ideas by over-intellectualising. They forget to apply their principles to everyday life, forget to think about human beings as real, warm, living people and become lost in pedantic arguments. Their perceptions become distorted and corrupt, tainting everything they see and touch. The book shows that they are often laughable but also dangerous to themselves and others.

Dealing with the supernatural

The supernatural reading

Ghost stories and supernatural tales have always had a place in folk tradition and popular fiction. You only have to think of the famous Hammer horror films and the endless Dracula/Frankenstein spin-offs to know that people enjoy them. High literature has sometimes tended to dismiss them, associating a rational approach with sophistication and education (markers of social success) and superstition with an uneducated, illogical frame of mind. Hogg was a victim of this literary preference since he was particularly good at writing serious supernatural stories but found that critics dismissed them as far-fetched. In this book he presents a supernatural story in a vivid, immediate way so that either it could be accepted as a story about the devil trapping a human soul *or* it could be treated as the imaginings of a mind that was literally abnormal, a mind that was going through the harrowing stages of a mental breakdown. He forestalls the critics by including an Editor to represent the rational viewpoint, pointing out and sometimes trying to explain those parts of the story that he finds incredible. The frame frees the author as he will no longer be held responsible for every inconsistency or supernatural detail. He has attempted to deflect the arguments of a critical reader, while retaining the mystery expected by a fan of the chiller. He has, moreover, created a highly sophisticated story that operates on a number of levels and still entertains.

The book is extremely effective as a version of the 'pact with evil' story that we meet in Shakespeare's *Macbeth*, Marlowe's *Doctor Faustus* or later in Oscar Wilde's *The Picture of Dorian Gray*. The Editor's Narrative prepares the ground and gives us details that Robert cannot. Robert's Memoir gives us a first-hand account to bring the events to life and make the devil speak direct to us. We are reminded how vulnerable each of us is

since this devil does not come breathing fire and brimstone: he
is personable, eloquent, an adept shape-changer and may pop up
in different places without our knowing. Of course, the devil
cannot enter until the actions of the characters give him leeway
and it is a neat turn that he should attach himself to a minister's
family, for it is the idea of God and heaven that presupposes the
existence of some evil alternative. Appropriately, the devil
preaches scripture back at his devout victims but it is only because their sin is so great, presuming to play God by judging
their fellows, that the devil has been roused at all.

In this reading, Gil-Martin has an objective existence and is
not simply a figment of Robert's imagination. This is confirmed
by those occasions on which other characters see him, for
example, when Arabella Logan and Bell Calvert see him in the
shape of George whom they both know to be dead. There are
also occasions when he actually possesses Robert's body as
when Robert loses track of time.

The psychological reading

When the book was 'rediscovered' in the twentieth century,
it was the psychological reading that first attracted interest
since Robert's story seems to be an amazingly accurate explor-
ation of a distraught mind experiencing paranoia, schizophrenia
and, eventually, complete collapse. The account could practically
have come out of the pages of a medical textbook and it is
possible that Hogg read some accounts of cases of schizophrenia
in Edinburgh newspapers. In a way Hogg himself knew what
it was like to have a double. The popular series of '*Noctes
Ambrosianae*' sketches in *Blackwood's Magazine* contained a
character, the Ettrick Shepherd, who was a caricature of James
Hogg. (The principal contributors were John Lockhart and John
Wilson. Wilson portrayed himself as the Editor of the series,
'Christopher North'.) Whatever the source, Hogg's material is
handled with care and, above all, compassion.

By this interpretation, it is clear that Robert's mind is unstable and that he has both a morbid jealousy of George and a
perverted attitude towards women and sexuality, since he has
been taught to see women as snares. (Presumably this is Wringhim Senior's self-justification for Robert's birth.) Though his
mother seems to exhibit some concern for him, he knows little
affection and is a solitary individual, whose illegitimacy causes
him to be the butt of jokes and speculation. To compensate for
this he embraces wholeheartedly the doctrines of his father's

harsh brand of Protestantism and freely indulges his hypocrisy and pride in the belief that, if he is one of the elect, he is superior to those around him who cause him most vexation. Until his salvation is assured, it also forces him to brood obsessively on the idea of sin.

The first stage of his breakdown occurs when, in his loneliness and rejection, he creates a being who offers him affection and bolsters his ego. It is therefore essential that this 'friend' be important but also devoted and able to accept the less attractive aspects of Robert's character. Robert can even externalise his bad, sinful impulses by projecting them on to his 'friend'. As Robert retreats into this state of mind, he finds it increasingly difficult to separate the real world from his invented world. He experiences further hallucinations (the mists and weapons) and gives way to his desires to elimiate those who threaten his happiness. Thus it is necessary for him to murder Blanchard since this moderate minister rejects the theories of absolute predestination that are Robert's 'proof' that his actions are right. His greed for position and his jealousy of George make the rest inevitable. It is his obsession with George that makes him 'see' George as a real manifestation at his side: perhaps he even wants to 'be' George or to cast him as his own 'good' side.

Part of him still realises that these actions and desires are wrong and he is literally no longer able to live with himself or the projection of himself that he has created. He has to blot out more and more actions from his memory (the girl's seduction and murder) and increasing dependence on alcohol makes this easy. His gradual disintegration is unavoidable and he slips into real madness as he wanders round the countryside, imagining that his 'good' and 'bad' sides are contesting for him and that he is being torn to pieces by demons.

One objection to this interpretation may be that others believe they see Gil-Martin. Sometimes we have only Robert's unreliable word for this, and Gil-Martin's 'shape-changing' may be accounted for by the fact that Robert projects him on to many different people — see the confusion with Blanchard (P: 139; O: 132). Elsewhere, the evidence comes to us by way of reported traditions and often the witnesses are themselves in an overwrought state, predisposed by stories of devils and so forth to believe they are seeing the impossible.

The real achievement, and this is true whichever reading one takes, is that Hogg leads us into the mind of a character who seems by all external measures simply evil and malicious. Then, gradually, by letting us see with that character's eyes, and listen to that character's thoughts, he contrives to make us feel pity and compassion for that character. The idea is humane and splendidly executed. Not only that, Hogg refuses to judge for us and will not act the critic or do our thinking for us. He deliberately sets difficult, paradoxical problems and moral dilemmas; he gives us the pieces and asks us to put the puzzle together; he suggests theories but in the end he asks us to put ourselves in his character's place and make choices. He asks all his readers to do what they must do in life but are rarely asked to do in fiction — make their own minds up.

NOTES

1   Undated letter from James Hogg's brother William, printed in Mrs Mary Garden's *Memorials of James Hogg the Ettrick Shepherd* (Paisley, 1903), p. 13. See also Elaine E. Petrie, 'Odd Characters: Traditional Informants in James Hogg's Family', *Scottish Literary Journal* (May 1983), pp. 30-41 for an account of Hogg's family as sources of information on folklore and local history.

2   'Dusty, or, Watie an' Geordie's Review of Politics; An Eclogue' in James Hogg, *Scottish Pastorals, Poems, Songs, &c.* (Edinburgh, 1801), pp. 9-24.

3   'Some Remarkable Passages in the Life of an Edinburgh Baillie, Written by Himself', *Tales of the Wars of Montrose*, 3 vols. (London, 1835), I, 1-297.

4   'The Adventures of Captain John Lochy, Written by Himself', *Altrive Tales: Collected Among the Peasantry of Scotland, and from Foreign Adventurers* (London, 1832), 1-141.

5   James Hogg, *Memoir of the Author's Life and Familiar Anecdotes of Sir Walter Scott*, ed. Douglas S. Mack (Edinburgh and London, 1972), p. 55.

BIBLIOGRAPHY

Works by James Hogg

Altrive Chapbooks, (Stirling: The James Hogg Society, 1984 —). (Selections of Hogg's work, published annually by the James Hogg Society.)

Anecdotes of Sir W. Scott, ed. Douglas S. Mack (Edinburgh: Scottish Academic Press, 1983).

The Brownie of Bodsbeck, ed. Douglas S. Mack (Edinburgh and London: Scottish Academic Press, 1976).

Memoir of the Author's Life and Familiar Anecdotes of Sir Walter Scott, ed. Douglas S. Mack (Edinburgh and London: Scottish Academic Press, 1972).

Highland Tours, ed. William F. Laughlan (Hawick: Byway Books, 1981).

The Private Memoirs and Confessions of A Justified Sinner, ed. John Carey (Oxford: Oxford University Press, The World's Classics, 1981).

The Private Memoirs and Confessions of A Justified Sinner, ed. John Wain (Harmondsworth, Middlesex: Penguin Books, 1983).

Selected Poems, ed. Douglas S. Mack (Oxford: Oxford University Press, 1970).

Selected Poems and Songs, ed. David Groves (Edinburgh: Scottish Academic Press, 1986).

Selected Stories and Sketches, ed. Douglas S. Mack (Edinburgh: Scottish Academic Press, 1982).

A Shepherd's Delight, ed. Judy Steel (Edinburgh: Canongate, 1985).

Tales of Love and Mystery, ed. David Groves (Edinburgh: Canongate, 1985).

The Three Perils of Man: War, Women and Witchcraft, ed. Douglas Gifford (Edinburgh and London: Scottish Academic Press, Scottish Classics Series, 1988).

Selected Works of Criticism

Douglas Gifford, *James Hogg* (Edinburgh: The Ramsay Head Press, 1976).

David Groves, 'James Hogg's *Confessions* and the Vale of Soul-Making' in *Studies in Scottish Fiction: Nineteenth Century*, ed. Horst W. Drescher and Joachim Schwend (Frankfurt am Main, Bern, New York: Verlag Peter Lang, 1986), pp. 29-41.

Gillian H. Hughes, ed., *Papers Given at the First James Hogg Society Conference* (Stirling: The James Hogg Society, 1983).

Gillian H. Hughes, ed., *Papers Given at the Second James Hogg Society Conference* (Edinburgh: The James Hogg Society, 1988).

Louis Simpson, *James Hogg: A Critical Study* (Edinburgh and London: Oliver and Boyd, 1962).

Nelson C. Smith, *James Hogg* (Boston: Twayne Publishers, 1980).

TEACHING AIDS

The Schools and Further Education Committee of the ASLS has produced a Lesson Pack of approximately 150 pages. It contains notes, units and workshops for the whole range of the secondary school. Some of the topics covered are:

The House with the Green Shutters, The Prime of Miss Jean Brodie, the poetry of Sydney Goodsir Smith, junior fiction and a substantial unit on language. (The pack is colour-coded for insertion into the Jordanhill Scottish Language and Literature Project).   £4.00

ASLS Commentary Cassettes

The following audio cassette commentaries have been produced and are now available:

Sunset Song by Douglas Young	£3.00
'The House with the Green Shutters' (A) Tone by Ian Campbell	£3.00
'The House with the Green Shutters' (B) Characterisation by Ian Campbell	£3.00
'The Silver Darlings' by Douglas Young	£3.00
R.L. Stevenson's 'Thrawn Janet' and 'Markheim' by Ian Campbell	£3.00
Hogg's 'Confessions of a Justified Sinner' by Douglas Gifford	£3.50
Fourteen Poems of Sorley Maclean by Iain Crichton Smith with readings by Sorley Maclean	£3.50
Three Poems of Burns by R.D.S. Jack ('Tam O'Shanter', 'John Anderson my Jo', and 'Holy Willie's Prayer')	£3.00
Seventeen Poems of Edwin Morgan by Roderick Watson with readings by Edwin Morgan	£3.50
Nineteen Poems of Norman MacCaig by Edwin Morgan with readings by Norman MacCaig	£3.50
Two Short Stories by Carl MacDougall by Elaine Petrie with readings by Carl MacDougall	£3.00